————— ✦ —————

God's Answers
for Your
Every Question
for Students

————— ✦ —————

ALBURY
PUBLISHING
TULSA, OKLAHOMA

God's Answers for Your Every Question for Students

ISBN 1-57778-041-8
Copyright © 1998 by ALBURY PUBLISHING
P. O. Box 470406
Tulsa, Oklahoma 74147-0406

CONTENTS

LORD, WHAT'S THE SECRET TO GOOD RELATIONSHIPS?

LORD, I NEED SOME ADVICE.
CAN YOU HELP ME?

TABLE OF CONTENTS

HOW CAN I KNOW YOU, GOD?

—◇—

Q: So much has changed
since the Bible was written.
How can I be sure its answers
still apply to my life today?

—◇—

A: Even if it was written in Scripture long
ago, you can be sure it's written for us.

ROMANS 15:4 THE MESSAGE

Every Scripture is God-breathed — given by
His inspiration.   2 TIMOTHY 3:16 AMP

"I tell you the truth, until heaven and earth
disappear, not the smallest letter, not the least
stroke of a pen, will by any means disappear
from the Law until everything is accomplished."

MATTHEW 5:18 NIV

"People are like grass that dies away; their beauty fades as quickly as the beauty of wildflowers.
The grass withers, and the flowers fall away. But
the word of the Lord will last forever."

1 PETER 1:24,25 NLT

Every part of Scripture is...useful one way or another — showing us truth, exposing our rebellion, correcting our mistakes, training us to live God's way.

2 TIMOTHY 3:16 THE MESSAGE

The word of God is living and powerful.

HEBREWS 4:12 NKJV

They are not just idle words for you — they are your life.

DEUTERONOMY 32:47 NIV

PRAYERS

Open my eyes to see the wonderful truths in your law.

PSALM 119:18 NLT

Forever, O Lord, your word stands firm in heaven. Your faithfulness extends to every generation, as enduring as the earth you created. Your laws remain true today, for everything serves your plans.

PSALM 119:89-91 NLT

From studying your laws, I found out long ago that you made them to last forever. All you say can be trusted; your teachings are true and will last forever.

PSALM 119:152,160 CEV

PROMISES

The law of the Lord is perfect, reviving the soul. The decrees of the Lord are trustworthy, making wise the simple. The commandments of the Lord are right, bringing joy to the heart. The commands of the Lord are clear, giving insight to life.

The laws of the Lord are true; each one is fair. They are more desirable than gold, even the finest gold. They are sweeter than honey, even honey dripping from the comb. They are a warning to those who hear them; there is great reward for those who obey them.

PSALM 19:7-11 NLT

"Heaven and earth will pass away, but My words will not pass away."

MATTHEW 24:35 NASB

Q: I'M LONELY, LORD.
WHAT'S THE SECRET TO
HAVING MORE FRIENDS?

A: Love from the center of who you are;
don't fake it. Run for dear life from evil; hold
on for dear life to good. Be good friends who
love deeply.

ROMANS 12:9,10 THE MESSAGE

This is my prayer: that your love will flourish
and that you will not only love much but well.
Learn to love appropriately. You need to use
your head and test your feelings so that your
love is sincere and intelligent, not sentimental
gush. Live...a life Jesus will be proud of.

PHILIPPIANS 1:9,10 THE MESSAGE

INSTRUCTIONS

Watch what God does, and then you do it,
like children who learn proper behavior from
their parents. Mostly what God does is love

you. Keep company with him and learn a life of love. Observe how Christ loved us. His love was not cautious but extravagant. He didn't love in order to get something from us but to give everything of himself to us. Love like that.

EPHESIANS 5:1,2 THE MESSAGE

Above all, love each other deeply, because love covers over a multitude of sins.

1 PETER 4:8 NIV

You must quit being angry, hateful, and evil. You must no longer say insulting or cruel things about others. And stop lying to each other. You have given up your old way of life with its habits. Each of you is now a new person. You are becoming more and more like your Creator.... So be gentle, kind, humble, meek, and patient. Put up with each other, and forgive anyone who does you wrong, just as Christ has forgiven you.

COLOSSIANS 3:8-10,12,13 CEV

Give as freely as you have received!

MATTHEW 10:8 NLT

Love is patient, love is kind. It does not envy, it does not boast, it is not proud. It is not rude, it is not self-seeking, it is not easily angered, it keeps no record of wrongs. Love does not delight in evil but rejoices with the truth. It always protects, always trusts, always hopes, always perseveres. Love never fails.

1 CORINTHIANS 13:4-8 NIV

Look for the best in each other, and always do your best to bring it out.

1 THESSALONIANS 5:15 THE MESSAGE

If someone is caught in a sin, you who are spiritual should restore him gently. GALATIANS 6:1 NIV

PROMISES

When the Holy Spirit controls our lives, he will produce this kind of fruit in us: love, joy, peace, patience, kindness, goodness, faithfulness, gentleness, and self-control.

GALATIANS 5:22,23 NLT

All who proclaim that Jesus is the Son of God have God living in them, and they live in God.... As we live in God, our love grows more perfect.... We love each other as a result of his loving us first.

1 JOHN 4:15,17,19 NLT

PRAYER

May the Lord make your love increase and overflow for each other and for everyone else, just as ours does for you.

1 THESSALONIANS 3:12 NIV

I pray that the Lord will guide you to be as loving as God and as patient as Christ.

2 THESSALONIANS 3:5 CEV

We pray that our Lord Jesus Christ and God our Father will encourage you and help you always to do and say the right thing.

2 THESSALONIANS 2:16,17 CEV

May your roots go down deep into the soil of God's marvelous love. And may you have the power to understand...how wide, how long, how high, and how deep his love really is. May you experience the love of Christ, though it is so great you will never fully understand it. Then you will be filled with the fullness of life and power that comes from God.

EPHESIANS 3:17-19 NLT

I pray that your love for each other will overflow more and more.... May you always be filled with the fruit of your salvation — those good things that are produced in your life by Jesus Christ.

PHILIPPIANS 1:9,11 NLT

EXAMPLE

God gave us the ultimate example of love:

This is how God showed his love for us: God sent his only Son into the world so we might live through him.... If God loved us like this, we certainly ought to love each other.

1 JOHN 4:9,11 THE MESSAGE

If we love each other, God lives in us, and his love has been brought to full expression through us.

1 JOHN 4:12 NLT

Q: WHAT SHOULD I LOOK FOR IN A FRIEND?

Pursue faith and love and peace, and enjoy the companionship of those who call on the Lord with pure hearts.

2 TIMOTHY 2:22 NLT

I am a friend to everyone who fears you. I am a friend to anyone who follows your orders.

PSALM 119:63 ICB

INSTRUCTIONS

Whoever spends time with wise people will become wise. But whoever makes friends with fools will suffer.

PROVERBS 13:20 ICB

Stay away from a foolish person. You won't learn anything from him. What makes a person wise is understanding what to do. But what makes a person foolish is dishonesty. Foolish people don't care if they sin. But honest people work at being right with others.

PROVERBS 14:7-9 ICB

Friends come and friends go, but a true friend sticks by you like family

PROVERBS 18:24 THE MESSAGE

The person who shuns the bitter moments of friends will be an outsider at their celebrations.

PROVERBS 14:10 THE MESSAGE

Do a favor and win a friend forever; nothing can untie that bond.

PROVERBS 18:19 THE MESSAGE

When you find a friend, don't outwear your welcome; show up at all hours and he'll soon get fed up.

PROVERBS 25:17 THE MESSAGE

Don't make friends with someone who easily gets angry. Don't spend time with someone who has a bad temper. If you do, you may learn to be like him. Then you will be in real danger.

PROVERBS 22:24,25 ICB

You must not associate with...anyone who calls himself a brother in Christ but who takes part in sexual sin, or is selfish, or worships idols, or lies about others, or gets drunk, or cheats people. Do not even eat with someone like that.

1 CORINTHIANS 5:11 ICB

Do not be fooled: "Bad friends will ruin good habits."

1 CORINTHIANS 15:33 NCV

Don't team up with those who are unbelievers. How can goodness be a partner with wickedness? How can light live with darkness? What harmony can there be between Christ and the Devil? How can a believer be a partner with an unbeliever? As God said: "I will live in them and walk among them. I will be their God, and they will be my people. Therefore, come out from them and separate yourselves from them, says the Lord. Don't touch their filthy things, and I will welcome you."

2 CORINTHIANS 6:14-17 NLT

If a fellow believer hurts you, go and tell him — work it out between the two of you. If he listens, you've made a friend."

MATTHEW 18:15 THE MESSAGE

Laugh with your happy friends when they're happy, share tears when they're down. Get along with each other; don't be stuck-up. Make friends with nobodies; don't be the great some-body.

ROMANS 12:15,16 THE MESSAGE

Become friends with God; he's already a friend with you.

2 CORINTHIANS 5:20 THE MESSAGE

Agree with each other; love each other; be deep-spirited friends.

PHILIPPIANS 2:2 THE MESSAGE

PROMISES

Happy is the person who doesn't listen to the wicked. He doesn't go where sinners go. He doesn't do what bad people do. He loves the Lord's teachings. He thinks about those teachings day and night. He is strong, like a tree planted by a river. It produces fruit in season. Its leaves don't die. Everything he does will succeed.

PSALM 1:1-3 ICB

For wisdom and truth will enter the very center of your being, filling your life with joy. You will be given the sense to stay away from evil men.

PROVERBS 2:10,11 TLB

Q: WHAT SHOULD I DO WHEN FRIENDS PRESSURE ME TO DO WRONG?

A: Ask the Lord Jesus Christ to help you live as you should, and don't make plans to enjoy evil.

ROMANS 13:14 TLB

INSTRUCTIONS

"Do not follow the crowd in doing wrong."

EXODUS 23:2 NIV

Don't sin because others do, but stay close to God.

1 TIMOTHY 5:22 CEV

Keep yourself pure.

1 TIMOTHY 5:22 NKJV

Run from temptations that capture young people. Always do the right thing.

2 TIMOTHY 2:22 CEV

Put on the full armor of God, so that when the

day of evil comes, you may be able to stand your ground.

EPHESIANS 6:13 NIV

Don't become partners with those who reject God. How can you make a partnership out of right and wrong? That's not partnership; that's war. Is light best friends with dark?... "So leave the corruption and compromise; leave it for good," says God. "Don't link up with those who will pollute you. I want you all for myself."

2 CORINTHIANS 6:14,17 THE MESSAGE

Let there be no sex sin, impurity or greed among you. Let no one be able to accuse you of any such things. Dirty stories, foul talk and coarse jokes — these are not for you. Instead, remind each other of God's goodness and be thankful. You can be sure of this: The Kingdom of Christ and of God will never belong to anyone who is impure or greedy, for a greedy person is really an idol worshiper — he loves and worships the good things of this life more than God.

Don't be fooled by those who try to excuse these sins, for the terrible wrath of God is upon all those who do them. Don't even associate with such people. For though once your heart was full of darkness, now it is full of light from the Lord, and your behavior should show it!

EPHESIANS 5:3-8 TLB

And so, dear brothers, I plead with you to give your bodies to God. Let them be a living sacrifice, holy — the kind he can accept. When you think of what he has done for you, is this too much to ask?

ROMANS 12:1 TLB

If a godly man compromises with the wicked, it is like polluting a fountain or muddying a spring.

PROVERBS 25:26 TLB

Keep away from every kind of evil.

1 THESSALONIANS 5:22 TLB

The fear of man brings a snare, but whoever leans on, trusts and puts his confidence in the Lord is safe and set on high.

PROVERBS 29:25 AMP

PROMISES

God blesses those people who are treated badly for doing right. They belong to the kingdom of heaven. God will bless you when people insult you, mistreat you, and tell all kinds of evil lies about you because of me. Be happy and excited! You will have a great reward in heaven. People did these same things to the prophets who lived long ago.

MATTHEW 5:10-12 CEV

I have not turned against him. I have not stopped following him.... The Lord God helps me. So I will not be ashamed. I will be determined. I know I will not be disgraced.

ISAIAH 50:5,7 ICB

PRAYERS

How can a young person live a pure life? He can do it by obeying your word. With all my heart I try to obey you, God. Don't let me break your commands. I have taken your words to heart so I would not sin against you. Lord, you should be praised. Teach me your demands.

PSALM 119:9-12 ICB

Lord, defend me. I have lived an innocent life. I trusted the Lord and never doubted. Lord, try me and test me. Look closely into my heart and mind. I see your love. I live by your truth. I do not spend time with liars. I do not make friends with people who hide their sin. I hate the company of evil people.... I have lived an innocent life. So save me and be kind to me.

PSALM 26:1-5,11 ICB

The Lord is my light and my salvation; whom shall I fear? The Lord is the strength of my life; of whom shall I be afraid?

PSALM 27:1 NKJV

If God is for us, who can be against us?

ROMANS 8:31 NKJV

May the God of peace himself make you entirely pure and devoted to God; and may your spirit and soul and body be kept strong and blameless until that day when our Lord Jesus Christ comes back again.

1 THESSALONIANS 5:23 TLB

EXAMPLES

Moses chose to side with God instead of with the people around him:

By faith Moses, when he had grown up,

refused to be known as the son of Pharaoh's daughter. He chose to be mistreated along with the people of God rather than to enjoy the pleasures of sin for a short time.

HEBREWS 11:24,25 NIV .

It was because he trusted God that he left the land of Egypt and wasn't afraid of the king's anger. Moses kept right on going; it seemed as though he could see God right there with him.

HEBREWS 11:27 TLB

Q: WHAT ABOUT WHEN FRIENDS
DRINK OR TAKE DRUGS? OR IF
THEY HANG OUT WITH THE
WRONG GROUP?

A: Don't copy the behavior and customs of
this world, but be a new and different person
with a fresh newness in all you do and think.
Then you will learn from your own experience
how his ways will really satisfy you.

ROMANS 12:2 TLB

INSTRUCTIONS

Don't follow the ways of the wicked. Don't do
what evil people do. Avoid their ways. Don't go
near what they do. Stay away from them and
keep on going. They cannot sleep until they do
evil. They cannot rest until they hurt someone.
They fill themselves with wickedness and cruelty
as if they were eating bread and drinking wine.
The way of the good person is like the light of

dawn. It grows brighter and brighter until it is full daylight. But the wicked are like those who stumble in the dark. They can't even see what has hurt them.

PROVERBS 4:14-19 ICB

Don't envy evil men but continue to reverence the Lord all the time, for surely you have a wonderful future ahead of you.... O my son, be wise and stay in God's paths; don't carouse with drunkards and gluttons, for they are on their way to poverty.

PROVERBS 23:17-20 TLB

Be very, very careful never to compromise...for if you do, you will soon be following their evil ways.

EXODUS 34:12 TLB

The night is far gone, the day of this return will soon be here. So quit the evil deeds of darkness and put on the armor of right living, as we who live in the daylight should! Be decent and true in everything you do so that all can approve your behavior. Don't spend your time in wild parties and getting drunk or in adultery and lust, or fighting, or jealousy. But ask the Lord Jesus Christ to help you live as you should, and don't make plans to enjoy evil.

ROMANS 13:12-14 TLB

You are not to keep company with anyone who claims to be a brother Christian but indulges in sexual sins, or is greedy, or is a swindler, or worships idols, or is a drunkard, or abusive. Don't even eat lunch with such a person.

1 CORINTHIANS 5:11 TLB

Wine gives false courage; hard liquor leads to brawls; what fools men are to let it master them, making them reel drunkenly down the street!

PROVERBS 20:1 TLB

You know well enough from your own experience that there are some acts of so-called freedom that destroy freedom. Offer yourselves to sin, for instance, and it's your last free act. But offer yourselves to the ways of God and the freedom never quits.

ROMANS 6:15,16 THE MESSAGE

Don't drink too much wine, for many evils lie along that path; be filled instead with the Holy Spirit and controlled by him.

EPHESIANS 5:18 TLB

For you are God's temple, the home of the living God, and God has said of you, "I will live

in them and walk among them, and I will be
their God and they shall be my people."

That is why the Lord has said, "Leave them;
separate yourselves from them; don't touch
their filthy things, and I will welcome you, and
be a Father to you, and you will be my sons
and daughters." 2 CORINTHIANS 6:16-18 TLB

Be with wise men and become wise. Be with
evil men and become evil. PROVERBS 13:20 TLB

Young men who are wise obey the law; a son
who is a member of a lawless gang is a shame
to his father. PROVERBS 28:7 TLB

If young toughs tell you, "Come and join us"
— turn your back on them! "We'll hide and
rob and kill," they say. "Good or bad, we'll treat
them all alike. And the loot we'll get! All kinds
of stuff! Come on, throw in your lot with us;
we'll split with you in equal shares."

Don't do it, son! Stay far from men like that,
for crime is their way of life, and murder is
their specialty.... They will die a violent death.

PROVERBS 1:10-16,19 TLB

The common bond of rebels is their guilt. The common bond of godly people is good will.

PROVERBS 14:9 TLB

Don't you realize that making friends with God's enemies — the evil pleasures of this world — makes you an enemy of God? I say it again, that if your aim is to enjoy the evil pleasure of the unsaved world, you cannot also be a friend of God.

JAMES 4:4 TLB

Stop loving this evil world and all that it offers you, for when you love these things you show that you do not really love God... This world is fading away, and these evil, forbidden things will go with it, but whoever keeps doing the will of God will live forever.

1 JOHN 2:15-17 TLB

Of course, your former friends will be very surprised when you don't eagerly join them anymore in the wicked things they do, and they will laugh at you in contempt and scorn. But just remember that they must face the Judge of all, living and dead; they will be punished for the way they have lived.

1 PETER 4:4,5 TLB

Dear brothers, you are only visitors here. Since your real home is in heaven I beg you to keep away from the evil pleasures of this world; they are not for you, for they fight against your very souls.

1 PETER 2:11 TLB

Before every man there lies a wide and pleasant road that seems right but ends in death.

PROVERBS 14:12 TLB

Take no part in the worthless pleasures of evil and darkness, but instead, rebuke and expose them.

EPHESIANS 5:11 TLB

Speak up for the right living that goes along with true Christianity.... And here you yourself must be an example to them of good deeds of every kind. Let everything you do reflect your love of the truth and the fact that you are in dead earnest about it.

TITUS 2:1,7 TLB

Be an example to the believers with your words, your actions, your love, your faith, and your pure life.

1 TIMOTHY 4:12 NCV

There's trouble ahead when you live only for

the approval of others, saying what flatters them, doing what indulges them. Popularity contests are not truth contests.... Your task is to be true, not popular.   LUKE 6:26 THE MESSAGE

Dear brothers, pattern your lives after mine and notice who else lives up to my example. For I have told you often before, and I say it again now with tears in my eyes, there are many who walk along the Christian road who are really enemies of the cross of Christ. Their future is eternal loss, for their god is their appetite: they are proud of what they should be ashamed of; and all they think about is this life here on earth. But our homeland is in heaven, where our Savior the Lord Jesus Christ is; and we are looking forward to his return from there.   PHILIPPIANS 3:17-20 TLB

PROMISE

The Lord grants wisdom! His every word is a treasure of knowledge and understanding. He grants good sense to the godly — his saints. He is their shield, protecting them and guarding their pathway. He shows how to distinguish right from wrong, how to find the right decision every time.

PROVERBS 2:6-9 TLB

The Lord...will bring to light what is hidden in darkness and will expose the motives of men's hearts.

1 CORINTHIANS 4:5 NIV

PRAYERS

For wisdom will enter your heart and knowledge will be pleasant to your soul; discretion will guard you, understanding will watch over you, to deliver you from the way of evil, from the man who speaks perverse things; from those who leave the paths of uprightness to walk in the ways of darkness...whose paths are crooked and who are devious in their ways.... So you will walk in the way of good men and keep to the paths of the righteous.

PROVERBS 2:10-13,15,20 NASB

You will show me the path of life; in Your presence is fullness of joy, at Your right hand there are pleasures for evermore.

PSALM 16:11 AMP

EXAMPLE

The people you spend time with can have a dramatic impact on your spiritual life, as King Solomon found out:

The Lord had said to the sons of Israel, "You shall not associate with them, neither shall they associate with you, for they will surely turn your heart away after their gods." Solomon held fast to these in love...his wives turned his heart away.... His heart was not wholly devoted to the Lord his God, as the heart of David his father had been.

1 KINGS 11:2,4 NASB

Q: WHAT ABOUT SEX? HOW FAR SHOULD I GO?

A: Above all else, guard your affections. For they influence everything else in your life. Spurn the careless kiss of a prostitute. Stay far from her. Look straight ahead; don't even turn your head to look. Watch your step. Stick to the path and be safe. Don't sidetrack; pull back your foot from danger.

PROVERBS 4:23-27 TLB

Honor marriage, and guard the sacredness of sexual intimacy between wife and husband. God draws a firm line against casual and illicit sex.

HEBREWS 13:4 THE MESSAGE

The commandment is a lamp, and the law a light; reproofs of instruction are the way of life, to keep you from the evil woman, from the flattering tongue of a seductress. Do not lust after her beauty in your heart, nor let her allure you with her eyelids.

Can a man take fire to his bosom, and his clothes not be burned? Can one walk on hot coals, and his feet not be seared?

PROVERBS 6:23-25,27,28 NKJV

You know well enough from your own experience that there are some acts of so-called freedom that destroy freedom. Offer yourselves to sin, for instance, and it's your last free act. But offer yourselves to the ways of God and the freedom never quits.

ROMANS 6:15,16 THE MESSAGE

Sexual sin is never right: our bodies were not made for that, but for the Lord, and the Lord wants to fill our bodies with himself.... Don't you realize that your bodies are actually parts and members of Christ? So should I take part of Christ and join him to a prostitute? Never! And don't you know that if a man joins himself to a prostitute she becomes a part of him and he becomes a part of her? For God tells us in the Scripture that in his sight the two become one person. But if you give yourself to the Lord, you and Christ are joined together as one person.

1 CORINTHIANS 6:13,15-17 TLB

That is why I say to run from sex sin. No other sin affects the body as this one does. When you sin this sin it is against your own body. Haven't you yet learned that your body is the home of the Holy Spirit God gave you, and that he lives within you? Your own body does not belong to you. For God has bought you with a great price. So use every part of your body to give glory back to God, because he owns it.

1 CORINTHIANS 6:18-20 TLB

Don't you realize that all of you together are the temple of God and that the Spirit of God lives in you? God will bring ruin upon anyone who ruins this temple. For God's temple is holy, and you Christians are that temple.

1 CORINTHIANS 3:16,17 NLT

Everyone who really believes this will try to stay pure because Christ is pure.

1 JOHN 3:3 TLB

Now you can have real love for everyone because your souls have been cleansed from self-ishness and hatred when you trusted Christ to save you; so see to it that you really do love each other...with all your hearts.

1 PETER 1:22 TLB

Be an example...with your words, your actions, your love, your faith, and your pure life.... Continue to read the Scriptures to the people, strengthen them, and teach them.... Be careful in your life and in your teaching. If you continue to live and teach rightly, you will save both yourself and those who listen to you.

1 TIMOTHY 4:12,13,16 NCV

Be their ideal; let them follow the way you teach and live; be a pattern for them in your love, your faith, and your clean thoughts.

1 TIMOTHY 4:12 TLB

Treat the older women as mothers, and the girls as your sisters, thinking only pure thoughts about them.

1 TIMOTHY 5:2 TLB

Avoid the very scenes of temptation.

PROVERBS 5:8 AMP

Abstain from all appearance of evil.

1 THESSALONIANS 5:22 KJV

If you notice that you are acting in ways inconsistent with what you believe...then you know that you're out of line. If the way you live isn't consistent with what you believe, then it's wrong.

ROMANS 14:23 THE MESSAGE

PROMISES

Happy is the person who doesn't listen to the wicked. He doesn't go where sinners go. He doesn't do what bad people do. He loves the Lord's teachings. He thinks about those teachings day and night.... Everything he does will succeed.

PSALM 1:1-3 ICB

Every part of Scripture is...useful one way or another — showing us truth, exposing our rebellion, correcting our mistakes, training us to live God's way.

2 TIMOTHY 3:16 THE MESSAGE

How can a young person live a pure life? He can do it by obeying your word. With all my heart I try to obey you, God. Don't let me break your commands.

PSALM 119:9,10 ICB

The eyes of the Lord watch over those who do right; his ears are open to their cries for help. But the Lord turns his face against those who do evil; he will erase their memory from the earth. The Lord hears his people when they call to him for help. He rescues them from all their troubles...from each and every one.

PSALM 34:15-17,19 NLT

Even if you think you can stand up to temptation, be careful not to fall. You are tempted in the same way that everyone else is tempted. But God can be trusted not to let you be tempted too much, and he will show you how to escape from your temptations.

1 CORINTHIANS 10:12,13 CEV

Now that the worst is over, we're pleased we can report that we've come out of this with conscience and faith intact, and can...face you with our heads held high. But it wasn't by any fancy footwork on our part. It was God who kept us focused on him, uncompromised.

2 CORINTHIANS 1:12 THE MESSAGE

God is working in you to make you willing and able to obey him.

PHILIPPIANS 2:13 CEV

PRAYERS

I have given them your word. And the world

hates them because they do not belong to the world, just as I do not. I'm not asking you to take them out of the world, but to keep them safe from the evil one. They are not part of this world any more than I am. Make them pure and holy by teaching them your words of truth. As you sent me into the world, I am sending them into the world. And I give myself entirely to you so they also might be entirely yours.

JOHN 17:14-19 NLT

May the God of peace himself make you entirely pure and devoted to God; and may your spirit and soul and body be kept strong and blameless until that day when our Lord Jesus Christ comes back again.

1 THESSALONIANS 5:23 TLB

Faithful is He Who is calling you [to Himself] and utterly trustworthy, and He will also do it [that is, fulfill His call by hallowing and keeping you].

1 THESSALONIANS 5:24 AMP

For wisdom will enter your heart and knowledge will be pleasant to your soul; discretion will guard you, understanding will watch over you, to deliver you from the way of evil...from those who leave the paths of uprightness to walk in the ways of darkness.... So you will walk in the way of good men and keep to the paths of the righteous.

PROVERBS 2:10-13,20 NASB

EXAMPLE

Joseph, a man of honor, refused to compromise his values and resisted the temptation to sin sexually:

It came about...that his master's wife looked with desire at Joseph, and she said, "Lie with me." But he refused and said..."How then could I do this great evil, and sin against God?" As she spoke to Joseph day after day, he did not listen to her to lie beside her or be with her. Now it happened one day...that she caught him by his garment, saying, "Lie with me!" And he left his garment in her hand and fled, and went outside.

GENESIS 39:7-12 NASB

Now flee from youthful lusts and pursue righteousness, faith, love and peace, with those who call on the Lord from a pure heart.

2 TIMOTHY 2:22 NASB

Q: WHAT IF THINGS HAVE ALREADY GONE TOO FAR?

A: Remember this — the wrong desires that come into your life aren't anything new and different. Many others have faced exactly the same problems before you. And no temptation is irresistible. You can trust God to keep the temptation from becoming so strong that you can't stand up against it, for he has promised this and will do what he says. He will show you how to escape temptation's power so that you can bear up patiently against it.

1 CORINTHIANS 10:13 TLB

INSTRUCTIONS

Let the wicked forsake his way, and the unrighteous man his thoughts; let him return to the Lord, and He will have mercy on him; and to our God, for He will abundantly pardon.

ISAIAH 55:7,12 NKJV

"I have set before you life and death, blessing and cursing; therefore choose life...that you may love the Lord your God, that you may obey His voice, and that you may cling to Him, for He is your life."

DEUTERONOMY 30:19,20 NKJV

He who conceals his sins does not prosper, but whoever confesses and renounces them finds mercy.

PROVERBS 28:13 NIV

What happiness for those whose guilt has been forgiven! What joys when sins are covered over! What relief for those who have confessed their sins and God has cleared their record. There was a time when I wouldn't admit what a sinner I was. But my dishonesty made me miserable and filled my days with frustration.

All day and all night your hand was heavy on me. My strength evaporated like water on a sunny day until I finally admitted all my sins to you and stopped trying to hide them. I said to myself, "I will confess them to the Lord." And you forgave me! All my guilt is gone.

Now I say that each believer should confess his

sins to God when he is aware of them, while there is time to be forgiven. Judgment will not touch him if he does. You are my hiding place from every storm of life; you even keep me from getting into trouble! Your surround me with songs of victory.

PSALM 32:1-7 TLB

It is for freedom that Christ has set us free. Stand firm, then, and do not let yourselves be burdened again by a yoke of slavery.... So I say, live by the Spirit, and you will not gratify the desires of the sinful nature.

GALATIANS 5:1,16 NIV

If we walk in the Light as He Himself is in the Light, we have fellowship with one another, and the blood of Jesus His Son cleanses us from all sin. If we say that we have no sin, we are deceiving ourselves, and the truth is not in us.

1 JOHN 1:7,8 NASB

But if we confess our sins to him, he can be depended on to forgive us and to cleanse us from every wrong. [And it is perfectly proper for God to do this for us because Christ died to wash away our sins.]

1 JOHN 1:9 TLB

For his mercy toward those who fear and honor him is as great as the height of the heavens above the earth. He has removed our sins as far away from us as the east is from the west. He is like a father to us, tender and sympathetic to those who reverence him. For he knows we are but dust.

PSALM 103:11-14 TLB

God is working in you to make you willing and able to obey him.

PHILIPPIANS 2:13 CEV

Cling tightly to your faith in Christ, and always keep your conscience clear. For some people have deliberately violated their consciences; as a result, their faith has been shipwrecked.

1 TIMOTHY 1:19 NLT

Be self-controlled and alert. Your enemy the devil prowls around like a roaring lion looking for someone to devour. Resist him, standing firm in the faith.

1 PETER 5:8,9 NIV

PRAYERS

Oh, wash me, cleanse me from this guilt. Let me be pure again.

PSALM 51:2 TLB

Have mercy on me, O God, according to your unfailing love; according to your great compassion blot out my transgressions. Wash away all my iniquity and cleanse me from my sin. For I know my transgressions, and my sin is always before me.

PSALM 51:1-3 NIV

Sprinkle me with the cleansing blood and I shall be clean again. Wash me and I shall be whiter than snow. And after you have punished me, give me back my joy again. Don't keep looking at my sins — erase them from your sight. Create in me a new, clean heart, O God, filled with clean thoughts and right desires.... Restore to me again the joy of your salvation, and make me willing to obey you.

PSALM 51:7-10,12 TLB

Wash me, and I will be whiter than snow.

PSALM 51:7 ICB

Now may our Lord Jesus Christ Himself, and our God and Father, who has loved us...comfort your hearts and establish you in every good word and work. The Lord is faithful, who will establish you and guard you from the evil one.

2 THESSALONIANS 2:16,17; 3:3 NKJV

EXAMPLE

Forgiveness requires repentance — you need to turn away from your sin and decide not to do it again:

The scribes and Pharisees brought to Him a woman caught in adultery. And when they had set her in the midst, they said to Him, "Teacher, this woman was caught in adultery, in the very act. Now Moses, in the law, commanded us that such should be stoned. But what do You say?"... He raised Himself up and said to them, "He who is without sin among you, let him throw a stone at her first."...

Then those who heard it, being convicted by their conscience, went out one by one.... Jesus was left alone, and the woman standing in the midst.... He said to her, "Woman, where are those accusers of yours? Has no one condemned you?" She said, "No one, Lord."...Jesus said to her, "Neither do I condemn you; go and sin no more."

JOHN 8:3-5,7,9-11 NKJV

Jesus forgives you, too. As you turn your heart away from your sin and choose to obey the Lord, He will help you and strengthen you in supernatural ways!

—∞—

Q: SO, WHAT'S THE BEST APPROACH TO DATING?

—∞—

A: Run from anything that gives you the evil thoughts that young men often have, but stay close to anything that makes you want to do right. Have faith and love, and enjoy the companionship of those who love the Lord and have pure hearts.

2 TIMOTHY 2:22 TLB

INSTRUCTIONS

Learn to put aside your own desires to that you will become patient and godly, gladly letting God have his way with you. This will make possible the next step, which is for you to enjoy other people and to like them, and finally you will grow to love them deeply.

2 PETER 1:6,7 TLB

Don't live to make a good impression on others. Be humble, thinking of others as better than yourself. Don't just think about your own affairs, but be interested in others, too, and in what they are doing.

PHILIPPIANS 2:3,4 TLB

Live no longer as the unsaved do, for they are
blinded and confused. Their closed hearts are
full of darkness; they are far away from the life
of God because they have shut their minds
against him, and they cannot understand his
ways. They don't care anymore about right and
wrong and have given themselves over to
impure ways. They stop at nothing, being dri-
ven by their evil minds and reckless lusts.

EPHESIANS 4:17-19 TLB

Avoid the very scenes of temptation.

PROVERBS 5:8 AMP

Be decent and true in everything you do so
that all can approve your behavior. Don't spend
your time in wild parties and getting drunk or
in adultery and lust, for fighting, or jealousy.

ROMANS 13:13 TLB

Having such great promises as these, dear
friends, let us turn away from everything wrong,
whether of body or spirit, and purify ourselves,
living in the wholesome fear of God, giving

ourselves to him alone.

2 CORINTHIANS 7:1 TLB

Now you can have real love for everyone because your souls have been cleansed from selfishness and hatred when you trusted Christ to save you; so see to it that you really do love each warmly, with all your hearts.

1 PETER 1:22 TLB

Love each other with brotherly affection and take delight in honoring each other.

ROMANS 12:10 TLB

Treat the older women as mothers, and the girls as your sisters, thinking only pure thoughts about them.

1 TIMOTHY 5:2 TLB

PROMISES

Trust in the Lord with all your heart and do not lean on your own understanding. In all your ways acknowledge Him, and He will make your paths straight. Do not be wise in your own eyes; fear the Lord and turn away from evil.

PROVERBS 3:5-7 NASB

Delight yourself also in the Lord, and He shall give you the desires of your heart.

Commit your way to the Lord, trust also in Him, and He shall bring it to pass.... Rest in the Lord, and wait patiently for Him.

PSALM 37:4,5,7 NKJV

The thing you should want most is God's kingdom and doing what God wants. Then all these other things you need will be given to you.

MATTHEW 6:33 NCV

PRAYERS

May God who gives patience, steadiness, and encouragement help you to live in complete harmony with each other — each with the attitude of Christ toward the other.
And then all of us can praise the Lord together with one voice, giving glory to God, the Father of our Lord Jesus Christ.

ROMANS 15:5,6 TLB

May the God of peace himself make you entirely pure and devoted to God; and may your spirit and soul and body be kept strong and blameless until that day when our Lord Jesus Christ comes back again.

1 THESSALONIANS 5:23 TLB

Q: LORD, AM I REALLY
SUPPOSED TO WAIT UNTIL YOU
PICK OUT A MATE FOR ME?

A: Parents can provide their sons with an
inheritance of houses and wealth, but only the
Lord can give an understanding wife.

PROVERBS 19:14 NLT

INSTRUCTIONS

And the Lord God said, "It isn't good for man
to be alone; I will make a companion for him, a
helper suited to his needs."

GENESIS 2:18 TLB

Every good thing given and every perfect
gift is from above, coming down from the
Father of lights.

JAMES 1:17 NASB

Your heavenly Father will give good things to
those who ask him!

MATTHEW 7:11 NCV

Remember, your Father knows exactly what

you need even before you ask him!

MATTHEW 6:8 TLB

You're blessed when you stay on course, walking steadily on the road revealed by God. You're blessed when you follow his directions.... That's right — you don't go off on your own; you walk straight along the road he set.

PSALM 119:1-3 THE MESSAGE

PROMISES

The Lord will guide you continually, and satisfy you with all good things. ISAIAH 58:11 TLB

Delight yourself in the Lord; and He will give you the desires of your heart. PSALM 37:4 NASB

He is close to all who call on him sincerely. He fulfills the desires of those who reverence and trust him; he hears their cries for help and rescues them. PSALM 145:18,19 TLB

The Lord gives grace and glory; no good thing does He withhold from those who walk uprightly. PSALM 84:11 NASB

Q: MY BEST FRIEND WON'T
TALK TO ME. WHAT
SHOULD I DO?

A: Always be willing to listen and slow to speak.

JAMES 1:19 NCV

INSTRUCTIONS

It is harder to win back the friendship of an offended brother than to capture a fortified city. His anger shuts you out like iron bars.

PROVERBS 18:19 TLB

A kind answer soothes angry feelings, but harsh words stir them up.

PROVERBS 15:1 CEV

Listen carefully to what you hear! The way you treat others will be the way you will be treated.

MARK 4:24 CEV

Let the wise listen and add to their learning.

PROVERBS 1:5 NIV

The purposes of a man's heart are deep waters, but a man of understanding draws them out.

PROVERBS 20:5 NIV

When others are happy, be happy with them. If they are sad, share their sorrow.

ROMANS 12:15 NLT

Stay away from foolish and stupid arguments, because you know they grow into quarrels. And a servant of the Lord must not quarrel but must be kind to everyone.

2 TIMOTHY 2:23,24 NCV

All of you should be of one mind, full of sympathy toward each other, loving one another with tender hearts and humble minds. Don't repay evil for evil. Don't retaliate when people say unkind things about you. Instead, pay them back with a blessing. That's what God wants you to do, and he will bless you for it.

1 PETER 3:8,9 NLT

Let's agree to use all our energy in getting along with each other. Help others with encouraging words; don't drag them down by finding fault.

ROMANS 14:19 THE MESSAGE

Say only what helps, each word a gift.

EPHESIANS 4:29 THE MESSAGE

"Be easy on people; you'll find life a lot easier."

LUKE 6:37 THE MESSAGE

"Don't pick on people, jump on their failures, criticize their faults — unless, of course, you want the same treatment. That critical spirit has a way of boomeranging."

MATTHEW 7:1 THE MESSAGE

Confess your sins to each other and pray for each other so that you can live together whole and healed. The prayer of a person living right with God is something powerful to be reckoned with.

JAMES 5:16 THE MESSAGE

He who covers his transgressions will not prosper, but whoever confesses and forsakes his sins shall obtain mercy.

PROVERBS 28:13 AMP

PROMISES

I will instruct you and teach you in the way you should go; I will counsel you and watch over you.

PSALM 32:8 NIV

"Go, and I, even I, will be with your mouth, and teach you what you are to say."

EXODUS 4:12 NASB

PRAYERS

"Teach me, and I will be quiet; show me where I have been wrong."

JOB 6:24 NIV

Show me your ways, O Lord, teach me your paths; guide me in your truth and teach me, for you are God my Savior, and my hope is in you all day long.... He guides the humble in what is right and teaches them his way.

PSALM 25:4,5,9 NIV

EXAMPLES

When believers withdraw from Jesus, He offers His fellowship and waits patiently for the door to open.

"Look! Here I stand at the door and knock. If you hear me calling and open the door, I will come in, and we will share a meal as friends. I will invite everyone who is victorious to sit with me on my throne."

REVELATION 3:20,21 NLT

Q: YOU WANT ME TO FORGIVE THEM? AFTER WHAT THEY DID TO ME?

A: Go ahead and be angry. You do well to be angry — but don't use your anger as fuel for revenge. And don't stay angry. Don't go to bed angry. Don't give the Devil that kind of foothold in your life.... Be gentle with one another, sensitive. Forgive one another as quickly and thoroughly as God in Christ forgave you.

EPHESIANS 4:26,27,32 THE MESSAGE

INSTRUCTIONS

Dear friends, never avenge yourselves. Leave that to God, for he has said that he will repay those who deserve it. [Don't take the law into your own hands.] Instead, feed your enemy if he is hungry. If he is thirsty give him something to drink and you will be "heaping coals of fire on his head." In other words, he will feel ashamed of himself for what he has done to you. Don't let evil get the upper hand but conquer evil by doing good.

ROMANS 12:19-21 TLB

If you forgive men when they sin against you, your heavenly Father will also forgive you. But if you do not forgive men their sins, your Father will not forgive your sins.

MATTHEW 6:14,15 NIV

"If your brother sins, rebuke him, and if he repents, forgive him. If he sins against you seven times in a day, and seven times comes back to you and says, 'I repent,' forgive him."

LUKE 17:3,4 NIV

"If another believer sins against you, go privately and point out the fault. If the other person listens and confesses it, you have won that person back."

MATTHEW 18:15 NLT

All of you should be in agreement, understanding each other...being kind and humble. Do not do wrong to repay a wrong, and do not insult to repay an insult. But repay with a blessing...that you might receive a blessing.

1 PETER 3:8,9 NCV

A man's wisdom gives him patience; it is to his glory to overlook an offense.

PROVERBS 19:11 NIV

If possible, so far as it depends on you, be at peace with all men.

ROMANS 12:18 NASB

PROMISES

God blesses those people who are merciful. They will be treated with mercy!

MATTHEW 5:7 CEV

Don't judge others, and God won't judge you. Don't be hard on others, and God won't be hard on you. Forgive others, and God will forgive you.

LUKE 6:37 CEV

PRAYERS

I pray that God will make you ready to obey him and that you will always be eager to do right. May Jesus help you do what pleases God.

HEBREWS 13:21 CEV

I can do everything with the help of Christ

who gives me the strength I need.

PHILIPPIANS 4:13 NLT

EXAMPLE

Peter asked Jesus, "Lord, how often should I forgive someone who sins against me?" In response, Jesus told the parable of "The Unforgiving Servant":

"The king summoned the man and said, 'You evil servant! I forgave your entire debt when you begged me for mercy. Shouldn't you be compelled to be merciful to your fellow servant who asked for mercy?' The king was furious and put the screws to the man until he paid back his entire debt. And that's exactly what my Father in heaven is going to do to each one of you who doesn't forgive unconditionally anyone who asks for mercy."

MATTHEW 18:32-35 THE MESSAGE

Q: MY FAMILY FIGHTS ALL THE
TIME. IS THERE A WAY TO STOP?

A: The servant of the Lord must not be
quarrelsome — fighting and contending.
Instead he must be kindly to every one and
mild-tempered — preserving the bond of peace.

2 TIMOTHY 2:24 AMP

INSTRUCTIONS

Always be willing to listen and slow to speak.
Do not become angry easily.

JAMES 1:19 ICB

When you do things, do not let selfishness or
pride be your guide. Instead, be humble and
give more honor to others than to yourselves.
Do not be interested only in your own life, but
be interested in the lives of others.

PHILIPPIANS 2:3,4 NCV

"Here is a simple, rule-of-thumb guide for
behavior: Ask yourself what you want people to

do for you, then grab the initiative and do it for them."

MATTHEW 7:12 THE MESSAGE

Don't use bad language. Say only what is good and helpful to those you are talking to, and what will give them a blessing.

EPHESIANS 4:29 TLB

A gentle answer will calm a person's anger. But an unkind answer will cause more anger.

PROVERBS 15:1 ICB

Get rid of all bitterness, rage and anger, brawling and slander, along with every form of malice. Be kind and compassionate to one another, forgiving each other, just as in Christ God forgave you. Be imitators of God, therefore, as dearly loved children and live a life of love.

EPHESIANS 4:31-5:2 NIV

For the whole law can be summed up in this one command: "Love your neighbor as yourself." But if instead of showing love among yourselves you are always biting and devouring one another, watch out! Beware of destroying one another.

GALATIANS 5:14,15 NLT

Let the peace of Christ keep you in tune with each other, in step with each other. None of this going off and doing your own thing. And cultivate thankfulness.

COLOSSIANS 3:15 THE MESSAGE

Do not do wrong to a person to pay him back for doing wrong to you. Or do not insult someone to pay him back for insulting you. But ask God to bless that person. Do this, because you yourselves were called to receive a blessing.... If you are always trying to do good, no one can really hurt you.

1 PETER 3:9,13 ICB

PROMISES

When a man's ways are pleasing to the Lord, He makes even his enemies to be at peace with him.

PROVERBS 16:7 NASB

Work hard at living in peace with others. The eyes of the Lord watch over those who do right, and his ears are open to their prayers. But the Lord turns his face against those who do evil.

1 PETER 3:11,12 NLT

PRAYERS

Now the God of peace...Make you perfect in every good work to do his will, working in you that which is wellpleasing in his sight, through Jesus Christ.

HEBREWS 13:20,21 KJV

"Love your enemies. Pray for those who hurt you. If you do this, then you will be true sons of your Father in heaven."

MATTHEW 5:44,45 ICB

EXAMPLE

What did Jesus do when men hurt Him? He prayed for them. It's not easy — but prayer works when nothing else will!

Jesus said, "Father, forgive them. They don't know what they are doing."

LUKE 23:34 ICB

"Love your enemies. Let them bring out the best in you, not the worst. When someone gives you a hard time, respond with the energies of prayer."

MATTHEW 5:44 THE MESSAGE

Q: THERE IS SOMEONE I CARE
ABOUT WHO REALLY NEEDS
TO KNOW YOU, LORD.
WHAT SHOULD I DO?

A: Everywhere we go we talk about Christ to all who will listen, warning them and teaching them as well as we know how. We want to be able to present each one to God, perfect because of what Christ has done for each of them.

COLOSSIANS 1:28 TLB

To this end I labor, struggling with all his energy, which so powerfully works in me.

COLOSSIANS 1:29 NIV

INSTRUCTIONS

If anybody asks why you believe as you do, be ready to tell him.

1 PETER 3:15 TLB

When you are with unbelievers, always make good use of the time. Be pleasant and hold their interest when you speak the message. Choose your words carefully and be ready to give answers to anyone who asks questions.

COLOSSIANS 4:5,6 CEV

The god of this age has blinded the minds of unbelievers, so that they cannot see the light of the gospel of the glory of Christ, who is the image of God.

2 CORINTHIANS 4:4 NIV

Pray without ceasing.

1 THESSALONIANS 5:17 NKJV

"To open their eyes so that they may turn from darkness to light and from the dominion of Satan to God, that they may receive forgiveness of sins and an inheritance among those who have been sanctified by faith in Me."

ACTS 26:18 NASB

Now this is the confidence that we have in Him, that if we ask anything according to His will, He hears us. And if we know that He hears us, whatever we ask, we know that we have the petitions that we have asked of Him.

1 JOHN 5:14,15 NKJV

"Behold, I have given you authority to tread on serpents and scorpions, and over all the power of the enemy, and nothing will injure you."

LUKE 10:19 NASB

"And I will give you the keys of the kingdom of heaven, and whatever you bind on earth will be bound in heaven, and whatever you loose on earth will be loosed in heaven."

MATTHEW 16:19 NKJV

PROMISES

"I was found by those who did not seek me; I revealed myself to those who did not ask for me."

ROMANS 10:20 NIV

For thus says the Lord God, "Behold, I Myself will search for My sheep and seek them out.... I will seek the lost, bring back the scattered, bind up the broken and strengthen the sick."

EZEKIEL 34:11,16 NASB

Thus says the Lord, In an acceptable and favorable time I have heard and answered you, and in a day of salvation I have helped you....

Saying to those who are bound, Come forth; to those who are in spiritual darkness, Show yourselves — come into the light.

ISAIAH 49:8,9 AMP

TO PRAY FOR THE LOST ONE

I...do not cease giving thanks for you, while making mention of you in my prayers; that the God of our Lord Jesus Christ, the Father of glory, may give to you a spirit of wisdom and of revelation in the knowledge of Him. I pray that the eyes of your heart may be enlightened, so that you will know what is the hope of His calling, what are the riches of the glory of His inheritance in the saints, and what is the surpassing greatness of His power toward us who believe.

EPHESIANS 1:15-19 NASB

My response is to get down on my knees before the Father.... I ask him to strengthen you by his Spirit...that Christ will live in you as you open the door and invite him in.

EPHESIANS 3:14,16,17 THE MESSAGE

Q: I HAVE TO MAKE A DECISION,
LORD — HOW CAN I KNOW
WHAT'S THE BEST CHOICE?

A: If you need wisdom — if you want to
know what God wants you to do — ask him,
and he will gladly tell you.

JAMES 1:5 NLT

INSTRUCTIONS

Call to me and I will answer you and tell you
great and unsearchable things you do not know.

JEREMIAH 33:3 NIV

My child, listen to me and treasure my
instructions. Tune your ears to wisdom, and
concentrate on understanding.... Search for
them as you would for lost money or hidden
treasure. Then you will understand what it
means to fear the Lord, and you will gain
knowledge of God.

PROVERBS 2:1,2,4,5 NLT

Trust God from the bottom of your heart.
Don't try to figure out everything on your own.
Listen for God's voice in everything you do,
everywhere you go. He's the one who will keep
you on track. Don't assume that you know it
all. Run to God!   PROVERBS 3:5-7 THE MESSAGE

All Scripture is inspired by God and is useful
to teach us what is true and to make us realize
what is wrong in our lives. It straightens us out
and teaches us to do what is right. It is God's
way of preparing us in every way, fully equipped
for every good thing God wants us to do.

2 TIMOTHY 3:16,17 NLT

PROMISES

I will instruct you and teach you in the way
you should go; I will counsel you and watch
over you.   PSALM 32:8 NIV

Your word is a lamp to my feet and a light to
my path.   PSALM 119:105 NKJV

The statutes of the Lord are trustworthy, making wise the simple. The precepts of the Lord

are right, giving joy to the heart. The commands of the Lord are radiant, giving light to the eyes.... By them is your servant warned; in keeping them there is great reward.

PSALM 19:7,8,11 NIV

PRAYERS

Send forth your light and your truth, let them guide me.

PSALM 43:3 NIV

Show me the path where I should walk, O Lord; point out the right road for me to follow. Lead me by your truth and teach me, for you are the God who saves me. All day long I put my hope in you.

PSALM 25:4,5 NLT

Teach me to do your will, for you are my God. May your gracious Spirit lead me forward on a firm footing.

PSALM 143:10 NLT

"Give me an understanding mind so that I can govern your people well and know the difference between what is right and what is wrong. For who by himself is able to carry such a heavy responsibility?"

1 KINGS 3:9 TLB

I will bless the Lord who guides me; even at night my heart instructs me.   PSALM 16:7 NLT

Your statutes are my delight; they are my counselors.   PSALM 119:24 NIV

EXAMPLE

When an enemy army came against Jehoshaphat, he sought the Lord for wisdom and guidance:

"We have no power to face this vast army that is attacking us. We do not know what to do, but our eyes are upon you." Then the Spirit of the Lord came upon Jahaziel.... He said..."This is what the Lord says to you: 'Do not be afraid or discouraged because of this vast army. For the battle is not yours, but God's. Go out to face them tomorrow, and the Lord will be with you.'"

2 CHRONICLES 20:12,14,15,17 NIV

———⟨∞⟩———

Q: I'M TIRED OF WORRYING
ABOUT EVERYTHING. HOW
CAN I QUIT?

———⟨∞⟩———

A: Don't fret or worry. Instead of worrying, pray. Let petitions and praises shape your worries into prayers, letting God know your concerns. Before you know it, a sense of God's wholeness, everything coming together for good, will come and settle you down. It's wonderful what happens when Christ displaces worry at the center of your life.

PHILIPPIANS 4:6-8 THE MESSAGE

INSTRUCTIONS

Cast your burden on the Lord, and He will sustain you; He will never permit the righteous to be moved.

PSALM 55:22 NKJV

Casting the whole of your care — all your anxieties, all your worries, all your concerns, once

and for all — on Him; for He cares for you
affectionately, and cares about you watchfully.

1 PETER 5:7 AMP

PROMISES

I am leaving you with a gift — peace of mind
and heart. And the peace I give isn't like the
peace the world gives. So don't be troubled or
afraid.

JOHN 14:27 NLT

The Lord is my light and my salvation; whom
shall I fear or dread? The Lord is the refuge and
stronghold of my life; of whom shall I be afraid?

PSALM 27:1 AMP

Those who live in the shelter of the Most
High will find rest in the shadow of the
Almighty. This I declare of the Lord; He alone
is my refuge, my place of safety; he is my God,
and I am trusting him.

PSALM 91:1,2 NLT

For he will rescue you from every trap and protect you from the fatal plague. He will shield
you with his wings.... His faithful promises are
your armor and protection. Do not be afraid of
the terrors of the night, nor fear the dangers of

the day.... Though a thousand fall at your side, though ten thousand are dying around you, these evils will not touch you.... For he orders his angels to protect you wherever you go.

PSALM 91:3-5,7,11 NLT

The Lord says, "I will rescue those who love me. I will protect those who trust in my name. When they call on me, I will answer; I will be with them in trouble. I will rescue them and honor them. I will satisfy them with a long life and give them my salvation." PSALM 91:14-16 NLT

But the Lord is faithful, and he will strengthen and protect you from the evil one.

2 THESSALONIANS 3:3 NIV

The angel of the Lord encamps around those who fear Him, and rescues them.

PSALM 34:7 NASB

PRAYERS

May the God of hope fill you with all joy and peace as you trust in him, so that you may overflow with hope by the power of the Holy Spirit.

ROMANS 15:13 NIV

In the multitude of my (anxious) thoughts within me, Your comforts cheer and delight my soul!

PSALM 94:19 AMP

EXAMPLE

During the night of the first Passover, a deadly plague killed the firstborn son in every Egyptian household. But as God's people trusted His word and obeyed His commands, they were protected from all harm:

Then Moses summoned all the elders of Israel and said to them, "Go at once and...slaughter the Passover lamb.... Put some of the blood on the top and on both sides of the doorframe. Not one of you shall go out the door of his house until morning. When the Lord goes through the land...he will see the blood...and will pass over that doorway, and he will not permit the destroyer to enter your houses and strike you down."

EXODUS 12:21-23 NIV

Q: LORD, I DON'T WANT
TO BE A CASUAL CHRISTIAN.
HOW CAN I BRING YOUR
POWER INTO MY WORLD?

A: Put your mind on your life with God.
The way to life — to God!— is vigorous and
requires your total attention.

LUKE 13:24 THE MESSAGE

INSTRUCTIONS

Never be lacking in zeal, but keep your spiritual fervor, serving the Lord.

ROMANS 12:11 NIV

Don't let anyone think little of you because you
are young. Be their ideal; let them follow the
way you teach and live; be a pattern for them in
your love, your faith, and your clean thoughts.

1 TIMOTHY 4:12 TLB

As Christ's soldier, do not let yourself become

tied up in the affairs of this life, for then you cannot satisfy the one who has enlisted you in his army. Follow the Lord's rules for doing his work, just as an athlete either follows the rules or is disqualified and wins no prize.

2 TIMOTHY 2:4,5 NLT

Jesus said, "You have been chosen to know the secrets about the kingdom of God.... The seed is God's message.... The seed that fell among the thorny weeds is like those who hear God's teaching, but they let the worries, riches, and pleasures of this life keep them from growing and producing good fruit." LUKE 8:10,11,14 NCV

"But the seed planted in the good earth represents those who hear the Word, embrace it, and produce a harvest beyond their wildest dreams."

MARK 4:20 THE MESSAGE

Don't love the world's ways. Don't love the world's goods. Love of the world squeezes out love for the Father.

1 JOHN 2:15 THE MESSAGE

Practically everything that goes on in the world — wanting your own way, wanting everything for yourself, wanting to appear important — has nothing to do with the Father. It just isolates you from him. The world and all its wanting, wanting, wanting is on the way out — but whoever does what God wants is set for eternity.

1 JOHN 2:16,17 THE MESSAGE

God has given each of us the ability to do certain things well. So if God has given you the ability to prophesy, speak out when you have faith that God is speaking through you. If your gift is that of serving others, serve them well. If you are a teacher, do a good job of teaching. If your gift is to encourage others, do it! If you have money, share it generously. If God has given you leadership ability, take the responsibility seriously. And if you have a gift for showing kindness to others, do it gladly.

ROMANS 12:6-8 NLT

There are different kinds of spiritual gifts, but they all come from the same Spirit. There are different ways to serve the same Lord, and we can each do different things. Yet the same God works in all of us and helps us in everything we do. The Spirit has given each of us a special way of serving others.

1 CORINTHIANS 12:4-7 CEV

For to one is given the word of wisdom through the Spirit, to another the word of knowledge through the same Spirit, to another faith by the same Spirit, to another gifts of healings by the same Spirit, to another the working of miracles, to another prophecy, to another discerning of spirits, to another different kinds of tongues, to another the interpretation of tongues. But one and the same Spirit works all these things, distributing to each one individually as He wills.

1 CORINTHIANS 12:8-11 NKJV

You will receive power when the Holy Spirit comes on you; and you will be my witnesses.

ACTS 1:8 NIV

"Truly, truly, I say to you, he who believes in Me, the works that I do, will he do also; and greater works than these he will do; because I go to the Father. Whatever you ask in My name, that will I do, so that the Father may be glorified in the Son. If you ask Me anything in My name, I will do it."

JOHN 14:12-14 NASB

PRAYER

Now the God of peace...equip you in every

good thing to do His will, working in us that which is pleasing in His sight, through Jesus Christ, to whom be the glory forever and ever. Amen.

HEBREWS 13:20,21 NASB

EXAMPLE

Jesus picked seventy of His followers and sent them out two by two ahead of Him to heal the sick and to proclaim that the kingdom of God has come.

Then the seventy returned with joy, saying, "Lord, even the demons are subject to us in Your name." And He said to them, "I saw Satan fall like lightning from heaven. Behold, I give you the authority...over all the power of the enemy, and nothing shall by any means hurt you."

LUKE 10:17-19 NKJV

"All the same, the great triumph is not in your authority over evil, but in God's authority over you and presence with you."

LUKE 10:20 THE MESSAGE

Q: How can I be a success?

A: "It's not possible for a person to succeed — I'm talking about eternal success — without heaven's help."

JOHN 3:27 THE MESSAGE

INSTRUCTIONS

In his heart a man plans his course, but the Lord determines his steps.

PROVERBS 16:9 NIV

You're blessed when you stay on course, walking steadily on the road revealed by God. You're blessed when you follow his directions, doing your best to find him. That's right — you don't go off on your own; you walk straight along the road he set.

PSALM 119:1-3 THE MESSAGE

Devote yourselves to prayer with an alert mind and a thankful heart.

COLOSSIANS 4:2 NLT

"This book of the law shall not depart from your mouth, but you shall meditate on it day and night, so that you may be careful to do according to all that is written in it; for then you will make your way prosperous, and then you will have success."

JOSHUA 1:8 NASB

"Be strong and do not give up, for your work will be rewarded."

2 CHRONICLES 15:7 NIV

The lazy person will not get what he wants. But a hard worker gets everything he wants.

PROVERBS 13:4 ICB

Refuse good advice and watch your plans fail; take good counsel and watch them succeed.

PROVERBS 15:22 THE MESSAGE

Form your purpose by asking for counsel, then carry it out using all the help you can get.

PROVERBS 20:18 THE MESSAGE

Do you see a man skilled in his work? That man will work for kings. He won't have to work for ordinary people.

PROVERBS 22:29 ICB

"Whoever wants to be great must become a servant."

MATTHEW 20:26 THE MESSAGE

A lazy life is an empty life.

PROVERBS 12:27 THE MESSAGE

PROMISES

"For I know the plans I have for you," declares the Lord, "plans to prosper you and not to harm you, plans to give you hope and a future. Then you will call upon me and come and pray to me, and I will listen to you. You will seek me and find me when you seek me with all your heart."

JEREMIAH 29:11-13 NIV

God can pour on the blessings in astonishing ways so that you're ready for anything and everything.

2 CORINTHIANS 9:8 THE MESSAGE

I can do all things through Christ, because he gives me strength.

PHILIPPIANS 4:13 NCV

We are God's workmanship, created in Christ Jesus to do good works, which God prepared in advance for us to do.

EPHESIANS 2:10 NIV

PRAYERS

I pray for good fortune in everything you do,

and for your good health — that your everyday affairs prosper, as well as your soul!

3 JOHN 2 THE MESSAGE

May the God of peace...equip you with all you need for doing his will. May he produce in you, through the power of Jesus Christ, all that is pleasing to him.

HEBREWS 13:20,21 NLT

EXAMPLE

God chose Solomon to build the temple in Jerusalem. His father, King David, encouraged him again and again, reminding him that the Lord would be with him as he worked to fulfill God's plan for his life.

David also said to Solomon his son, "Be strong and courageous, and do the work. Do not be afraid or discouraged, for the Lord God, my God, is with you. He will not fail you or forsake you until all the work for the service of the temple of the Lord is finished.

1 CHRONICLES 28:20 NIV

———◇◇◇———

Q: IS THERE A WAY TO BE HAPPY NO MATTER WHAT HAPPENS?

———◇◇◇———

A: You are my hiding place! You protect me from trouble, and you put songs in my heart.

PSALM 32:7 CEV

I was pushed back and about to fall, but the Lord helped me. The Lord is my strength and my song; he has become my salvation.

PSALM 118:13,14 NIV

INSTRUCTIONS

Let all who take refuge in you be glad; let them ever sing for joy. Spread your protection over them, that those who love your name may rejoice in you. For surely, O Lord, you bless the righteous; you surround them with your favor as with a shield.

PSALM 5:11,12 NIV

Let the godly rejoice. Let them be glad in

God's presence. Let them be filled with joy.
Sing praises to God and to his name! Sing
loud praises to him who rides the clouds. His
name is the Lord — rejoice in his presence!

PSALM 68:3,4 NLT

Rejoice in the Lord always. Again I will say,
rejoice!

PHILIPPIANS 4:4 NKJV

Speak to each other with psalms, hymns, and
spiritual songs, singing and making music in
your hearts to the Lord. Always give thanks to
God the Father for everything.

EPHESIANS 5:19,20 NCV

Do everything without complaining.

PHILIPPIANS 2:14 NCV

And you shall rejoice before the Lord your
God in all that you undertake.

DEUTERONOMY 12:18 AMP

Whenever trouble comes your way, let it be an
opportunity for joy. For when your faith is test-
ed, your endurance has a chance to grow. So let
it grow, for when your endurance is fully devel-
oped, you will be strong in character and ready

for anything.

JAMES 1:2-4 NLT

Though you have not seen him, you love him; and even though you do not see him now, you believe in him and are filled with an inexpress-ible and glorious joy.

1 PETER 1:8 NIV

PRAYERS

I will greatly rejoice in the Lord, my soul shall be joyful in my God; for He has clothed me with the garments of salvation, He has covered me with the robe of righteousness, as...a bride adorns herself with her jewels.

ISAIAH 61:10 NKJV

It is good to say, "Thank you" to the Lord, to sing praises to the God who is above all gods. Every morning tell him, "Thank you for your kindness," and every evening rejoice in all his faithfulness. You have done so much for me, O Lord. No wonder I am glad! I sing for joy.

PSALM 92:1,2,4 TLB

Why are you cast down, O my inner self? And why should you moan over me and be disquieted within me? Hope in God and wait expectantly for Him; for I shall yet praise Him, Who is the help of my [sad] countenance, and my God.

PSALM 43:5 AMP

PROMISES

Though a righteous man falls seven times, he rises again.

PROVERBS 24:16 NIV

Blessed is the man who endures temptation; for when he has been approved, he will receive the crown of life which the Lord has promised to those who love Him.

JAMES 1:12 NKJV

EXAMPLE

Habakkuk declares that his joy is not based on his circumstances but in his God:

Fig trees may not grow figs. There may be no grapes on the vines. There may be no olives growing on the trees. There may be no food growing in the fields. There may be no sheep in the pens. There may be no cattle in the barns. But I will still be glad in the Lord. I will rejoice in God my Savior. The Lord God gives me my strength.

HABAKKUK 3:17-19 ICB

---◆◆◆---

Q: I HAVE MADE A BIG MISTAKE,
AND I FEEL REALLY BAD.
WILL YOU FORGIVE ME, LORD?

---◆◆◆---

A: I'm glad...that you were jarred into turning things around. You let the distress bring you to God, not drive you from him. The result was all gain, no loss.

2 CORINTHIANS 7:9 THE MESSAGE

God can use sorrow in our lives to help us turn away from sin.... Just see what this godly sorrow produced in you!...You showed that you have done everything you could to make things right.

2 CORINTHIANS 7:10,11 NLT

INSTRUCTIONS

He who conceals his sins does not prosper, but whoever confesses and renounces them finds mercy.

PROVERBS 28:13 NIV

Blessed is he whose transgressions are forgiven, whose sins are covered. Blessed is the man whose sin the Lord does not count against him.

PSALM 32:1,2 NIV

There was a time when I wouldn't admit what a sinner I was. But my dishonesty made me miserable and filled my days with frustration.... I finally admitted all my sins to you and stopped trying to hide them. I said to myself, "I will confess them to the Lord." And you forgave me! All my guilt is gone.

PSALM 32:3,5 TLB

Confess your sins to each other and pray for each other so that you can live together whole and healed. The prayer of a person living right with God is something powerful to be reckoned with.

JAMES 5:16 THE MESSAGE

PROMISES

Is anyone crying for help? God is listening, ready to rescue you. If your heart is broken, you'll find God right there.

PSALM 34:17,18 THE MESSAGE

He heals the heartbroken and bandages their wounds.

PSALM 147:3 THE MESSAGE

If we walk in the Light as He Himself is in the Light, we have fellowship with one another, and the blood of Jesus His Son cleanses us from all sin. If we say that we have no sin, we are deceiving ourselves and the truth is not in us. If we confess our sins, He is faithful and righteous to forgive us our sins and to cleanse us from all unrighteousness.

1 JOHN 1:7-9 NASB

As far as the east is from the west, so far has he removed our transgressions from us.

PSALM 103:12 NIV

PRAYERS

Have mercy on me, O God, according to your unfailing love; according to your great compassion blot out my transgressions. Wash away all my iniquity and cleanse me from my sin. For I know my transgressions, and my sin is always before me.

PSALM 51:1-3 NIV

Create in me a pure heart, O God, and renew

a steadfast spirit within me.

PSALM 51:10 NIV

Now may our Lord Jesus Christ Himself, and our God and Father, who has loved us...comfort your hearts and establish you in every good word and work.... The Lord is faithful, who will establish you and guard you from the evil one.

2 THESSALONIANS 2:16,17; 3:3 NKJV

EXAMPLE

King David is an example of a man who received God's forgiveness and then forgave himself:

I said, "I will confess my transgressions to the Lord" and You forgave the iniquity of my sin.... You are my hiding place; You shall preserve me from trouble; You shall surround me with songs of deliverance. Selah.... Be glad in the Lord and rejoice, you righteous; and shout for joy, all you upright in heart!

PSALM 32:5,7,11 NKJV

God's gift of righteousness was so real to David that he was able to once again see himself as one of the righteous, as one who was upright in heart. And the revelation of God's mercy made him shout for joy!

---◆---

Q: I KEEP MESSING UP, LORD!
HOW CAN I CHANGE?

---◆---

A: God is working in you, giving you the desire to obey him and the power to do what pleases him.

PHILIPPIANS 2:13 NLT

We are God's masterpiece. He has created us anew in Christ Jesus, so that we can do the good things he planned for us long ago.

EPHESIANS 2:10 NLT

INSTRUCTIONS

Faith comes by hearing, and hearing by the word of God.

ROMANS 10:17 NKJV

As newborn babes, desire the pure milk of the word, that you may grow thereby.

1 PETER 2:2 NKJV

For you have been born again not of seed which is perishable but imperishable, that is, through the living and enduring word of God.

1 PETER 1:23 NASB

All Scripture is given by God and is useful for teaching, for showing people what is wrong in their lives, for correcting faults, and for teaching how to live right. Using the Scriptures, the person who serves God will be capable, having all that is needed to do every good work.

2 TIMOTHY 3:16,17 NCV

And so, dear brothers and sisters, I plead with you to give your bodies to God. Let them be a living and holy sacrifice — the kind he will accept. When you think of what he has done for you, is this too much to ask? Don't copy the behavior and customs of this world, but let God transform you into a new person by changing the way you think. Then you will know what God wants you to do, and you will know how good and pleasing and perfect his will really is.

ROMANS 12:1,2 NLT

Do not merely listen to the word, and so deceive yourselves. Do what it says.

JAMES 1:22 NIV

"Everyone who hears these words of Mine
and acts upon them, may be compared to a
wise man who built his house upon the rock.
And the rain fell, and the floods came, and the
winds blew and slammed against that house;
and yet it did not fall, for it had been founded
upon the rock."

MATTHEW 7:24-27 NASB

"This Book of the Law shall not depart from
your mouth, but you shall meditate in it day
and night, that you may observe to do according
to all that is written in it. For then you will
make your way prosperous, and then you will
have good success."

JOSHUA 1:8 NKJV

PROMISES

If anyone is in Christ, he is a new creation; old
things have passed away; behold, all things
have become new.

2 CORINTHIANS 5:17 NKJV

God gives us what it takes to do all that we do.

2 CORINTHIANS 3:5 CEV

In the past you were slaves to sin — sin

controlled you. But thank God, you fully obeyed the things that you were taught. You were made free from sin, and now you are slaves to goodness.

ROMANS 6:17,18 NCV

And having been set free from sin, you have become the servants of righteousness.

ROMANS 6:18 AMP

PRAYERS

We keep on praying for you that our God...will make you as good as you wish you could be! — rewarding your faith with his power. Then everyone will be praising the name of the Lord Jesus Christ because of the results they see in you; and your greatest glory will be that you belong to him. The tender mercy of our God and of the Lord Jesus Christ has made all this possible for you.

2 THESSALONIANS 1:11,12 TLB

We have kept on praying and asking God to help you understand what he wants you to do; asking him to make you wise about spiritual things; and asking that the way you live will always please the Lord and honor him, so that you will always be doing good, kind things for others, while all the time you are learning to know God better and better. We are praying, too, that you will be filled with his mighty, glorious strength so that you can keep going no matter what happens — always full of the joy of the Lord.

COLOSSIANS 1:9-11 TLB

EXAMPLE

The Apostle Paul experienced a tremendous turnaround in his life as he received God's grace:

Even though I was once a blasphemer and a persecutor and a violent man, I was shown mercy because I acted in ignorance and unbelief. The grace of our Lord was poured out on me abundantly, along with the faith and love that are in Christ Jesus.

1 TIMOTHY 1:13,14 NIV

Jesus Christ came into the world to save sinners. I'm proof — Public Sinner Number One — of someone who could never have made it apart from sheer mercy. And now he shows me off — evidence of his endless patience — to those who are right on the edge of trusting him forever.

1 TIMOTHY 1:15,16 THE MESSAGE

Q: WHAT SHOULD I DO WHEN I'M TEMPTED TO SIN?

A: "I have set before you life and death, blessing and cursing; therefore choose life, that both you and your descendants may live; that you may love the Lord your God, that you may obey His voice, and that you may cling to Him, for He is your life."

DEUTERONOMY 30:19,20 NKJV

Remember this — the wrong desires that come into your life aren't anything new and different. Many others have faced exactly the same problems before you. And no temptation is irresistible. You can trust God to keep the temptation from becoming so strong that you can't stand up against it, for he has promised this and will do what he says. He will show you how to escape temptation's power so that you can bear up patiently against it.

1 CORINTHIANS 10:13 TLB

INSTRUCTIONS

Happy is the man who doesn't give in and do wrong when he is tempted, for afterwards he will get as his reward the crown of life that God has promised those who love him.

And remember, when someone wants to do wrong it is never God who is tempting him, for God never wants to do wrong and never tempts anyone else to do it. Temptation is the pull of man's own evil thoughts and wishes. These evil thoughts lead to evil actions.

JAMES 1:12-15 TLB

If you want a happy life and good days, keep your tongue from speaking evil, and keep your lips from telling lies. Turn away from evil and do good. Work hard at living in peace with others. The eyes of the Lord watch over those who do right, and his ears are open to their prayers. But the Lord turns his face against those who do evil.

1 PETER 3:10-12 NLT

The good man does not escape all troubles — he has them too. But the Lord helps him in each and every one.

PSALM 34:19 TLB

The steps of good men are directed by the Lord. He delights in each step they take. If they fall it isn't fatal, for the Lord holds them with his hand.

PSALM 37:23,24 TLB

Be on your guard and stay awake. Your enemy, the devil, is like a roaring lion, sneaking around to find someone to attack. But you must resist the devil and stay strong in your faith.

1 PETER 5:8,9 CEV

Our fight is not against people on earth but...against the spiritual powers of evil in the heavenly world. That is why you need to put on God's full armor. Then on the day of evil you will be able to stand strong. And when you have finished the whole fight, you will still be standing. So stand strong, with the belt of truth tied around your waist and the protection of right living on your chest. On your feet wear the Good News of peace.... And also use the shield of faith with which you can stop all the burning arrows of the Evil One. Accept God's salvation as your helmet, and take the sword of the Spirit, which is the word of God. Pray in the Spirit at all times.

EPHESIANS 6:12-18 NCV

You are strong, and the word of God lives in you, and you have overcome the evil one.

1 JOHN 2:14 NIV

How we thank God, who gives us victory over sin and death through Jesus Christ our Lord!

1 CORINTHIANS 15:57 NLT

For every child of God can obey him, defeating sin and evil pleasure by trusting Christ to help him.

1 JOHN 5:4 TLB

PROMISES

The Lord knows how to deliver the godly out of temptations.

2 PETER 2:9 NKJV

The Lord is faithful, and He will strengthen and protect you from the evil one.

2 THESSALONIANS 3:3 NASB

You are from God, little children, and have overcome them; because greater is He who is in you than he who is in the world.

1 JOHN 4:4 NASB

I can do everything with the help of Christ

who gives me the strength I need.

PHILIPPIANS 4:13 NLT

God began doing a good work in you. And he will continue it until it is finished when Jesus Christ comes again. I am sure of that.

PHILIPPIANS 1:6 ICB

Now glory be to God! By his mighty power at work within us, he is able to accomplish infinitely more than we would ever dare to ask or hope.

EPHESIANS 3:20 NLT

God can do anything, you know — far more than you could ever imagine or guess or request in your wildest dreams! He does it not by pushing us around but by working within us, his Spirit deeply and gently within us.

EPHESIANS 3:20 THE MESSAGE

[Not in your own strength] for it is God Who is all the while effectually at work in you — energizing and creating in you the power and desire — both to will and to work for His good pleasure and satisfaction and delight.

PHILIPPIANS 2:13 AMP

Anyone who meets a testing challenge head-on and manages to stick it out is mighty fortunate. For such persons loyally in love with God, the reward is life and more life.

JAMES 1:12 THE MESSAGE

PRAYERS

Deliver us from the evil one.

MATTHEW 6:13 NKJV

The Lord will deliver me from every evil work and preserve me for His heavenly kingdom.

2 TIMOTHY 4:18 NKJV

We always pray for you, asking our God to help you live the kind of life he called you to live.

2 THESSALONIANS 1:11 NCV

Then...you will bring honor to the name of our Lord Jesus, and he will bring honor to you.

2 THESSALONIANS 1:12 CEV

The Lord is faithful and He will strengthen [you] and set you on a firm foundation and guard you from the evil [one].

2 THESSALONIANS 3:3 AMP

Q: I LOST MY TEMPER — AGAIN.
CAN YOU HELP ME, LORD?

A: Those who control their anger have great understanding; those with a hasty temper will make mistakes.

PROVERBS 14:29 NLT

Slowness to anger makes for deep understanding; a quick-tempered person stockpiles stupidity.

PROVERBS 14:29 THE MESSAGE

INSTRUCTIONS

Put these things out of your life: anger, bad temper, doing or saying things to hurt others, and using evil words when you talk.

COLOSSIANS 3:8 NCV

I promise you that on the day of judgment, everyone will have to account for every careless word they have spoken.

MATTHEW 12:36 CEV

"You're familiar with the command to the

ancients, 'Do not murder.' I'm telling you that anyone who is so much as angry with a brother or sister is guilty of murder.... The simple moral fact is that words kill."

MATTHEW 5:21,22 THE MESSAGE

"Don't sin by letting anger gain control over you." Don't let the sun go down while you are still angry, for anger gives a mighty foothold to the Devil.

EPHESIANS 4:26,27 NLT

When you talk, do not say harmful things, but say what people need — words that will help others become stronger. Then what you say will do good to those who listen to you.

EPHESIANS 4:29 NCV

Let every man be quick to hear, (a ready listener,) slow to speak, slow to take offense and to get angry.

JAMES 1:19 AMP

God's righteousness doesn't grow from human anger.

JAMES 1:20 THE MESSAGE

Do not be overcome by evil, but overcome evil with good.

ROMANS 12:21 NASB

Since God chose you to be the holy people whom he loves, you must clothe yourselves with tenderhearted mercy, kindness, humility, gentleness, and patience. You must make allowance for each other's faults and forgive the person who offends you. Remember, the Lord forgave you, so you must forgive others.

COLOSSIANS 3:12,13 NLT

PROMISES

We have everything we need to live a life that pleases God. It was all given to us by God's own power, when we learned that he had invited us to share in his wonderful goodness. God made great and marvelous promises, so that his nature would become part of us.

2 PETER 1:3,4 CEV

So make every effort to apply the benefits of these promises to your life…. Knowing God leads to self-control. Self-control leads to patient endurance, and patient endurance leads to godliness.

2 PETER 1:5,6 NLT

"Blessed are the merciful, for they shall receive mercy…. Blessed are the peacemakers, for they shall be called sons of God."

MATTHEW 5:7,9 NASB

Delight yourself also in the Lord, and He will give you the desires and secret petitions of your heart. Commit your way to the Lord — roll and repose [each care of] your load on Him; trust (lean on, rely on and be confident) also in Him, and He will bring it to pass. Be still and rest in the Lord; wait for Him, and patiently stay yourself upon Him.... Cease from anger and forsake wrath; fret not yourself; it tends only to evil-doing.... But the meek [in the end] shall inherit the earth, and shall delight themselves in the abundance of peace.

PSALM 37:4,5,7,8,11 AMP

PRAYER

Who can understand his errors? Cleanse me from secret faults. Keep back Your servant also from presumptuous sins; let them not have dominion over me. Then I shall be blameless, and I shall be innocent of great transgression. Let the words of my mouth and the meditation of my heart be acceptable in Your sight, O

Lord, my strength and my Redeemer.

PSALM 19:12-14 NKJV

We always pray that God will show you everything he wants you to do and that you may have all the wisdom and understanding that his Spirit gives. Then you will live a life that honors the Lord.

COLOSSIANS 1:9,10 CEV

EXAMPLE

Our Heavenly Father sees our failures and weakness yet responds with mercy and not anger.

The Lord is merciful and gracious, slow to anger, and plenteous in mercy and loving-kindness. He will not always chide or be contending, neither will He keep His anger for ever or hold a grudge. He has not dealt with us after our sins, nor rewarded us according to our iniquities.... As a father loves and pities his children, so the Lord loves and pities those who fear Him — with reverence, worship and awe. For He knows our frame; He [earnestly] remembers and imprints [on His heart] that we are dust.

PSALM 103:8-10,13,14 AMP

Q: IT'S BEEN A BAD DAY, LORD. DO YOU HAVE ANY WORDS OF ENCOURAGEMENT FOR ME?

A: "Do not fear, for I am with you; do not anxiously look about you, for I am your God. I will strengthen you, surely I will help you, surely I will uphold you with My righteous right hand."

ISAIAH 41:10 NASB

Whatever I have, wherever I am, I can make it through anything in the One who makes me who I am.

PHILIPPIANS 4:13 THE MESSAGE

INSTRUCTIONS

Cast your burden upon the Lord and He will sustain you; He will never allow the righteous to be shaken.

PSALM 55:22 NASB

Fix your thoughts on what is true and good and right. Think about things that are pure and lovely, and dwell on the fine, good things in others. Think about all you can praise God for and be glad about. Keep putting into practice all you learned from me...and the God of peace will be with you.

PHILIPPIANS 4:8,9 TLB

Let the peace of heart that comes from Christ be always present in your hearts and lives.... And always be thankful.

COLOSSIANS 3:15 TLB

Nothing you do for him is a waste of time or effort.

1 CORINTHIANS 15:58 THE MESSAGE

We live by faith, not by sight.

2 CORINTHIANS 5:7 NIV

Now faith is being sure of what we hope for and certain of what we do not see.

HEBREWS 11:1 NIV

Even though on the outside it often looks like things are falling apart on us, on the inside, where God is making new life, not a day goes by without his unfolding grace.

2 CORINTHIANS 4:16 THE MESSAGE

In times of trouble, God is with us, and when

we are knocked down, we get up again.

2 CORINTHIANS 4:9 CEV

Instead of trusting in our own strength or wits to get out of it, we were forced to trust God totally — not a bad idea since he's the God who raises the dead!

2 CORINTHIANS 1:9 THE MESSAGE

PROMISES

And I am sure that God, who began the good work within you, will continue his work until it is finally finished on that day when Christ Jesus comes back again.

PHILIPPIANS 1:6 NLT

Be energetic in your life of salvation, reverent and sensitive before God. That energy is God's energy, an energy deep within you, God himself willing and working at what will give him the most pleasure.

PHILIPPIANS 2:12,13 THE MESSAGE

He gives power to the faint and weary, and to him who has no might He increases strength — causing it to multiply and making it abound.

ISAIAH 40:29 AMP

PRAYERS

We pray that you'll have the strength to stick it out over the long haul...strength that endures the unendurable and spills over into joy.

COLOSSIANS 1:11,12 THE MESSAGE

We wait in hope for the Lord; he is our help and our shield. In him our hearts rejoice, for we trust in his holy name. May your unfailing love rest upon us, O Lord, even as we put our hope in you.

PSALM 33:20-22 NIV

I wait for the Lord, my soul does wait, and in His word do I hope. My soul waits for the Lord more than the watchmen for the morning.... Hope in the Lord; for with the Lord there is lovingkindness, and with Him is abundant redemption.

PSALM 130:5-7 NASB

When You said, "Seek My face," my heart said to You, "Your face, O Lord, I seek."
I would have despaired unless I had believed that I would see the goodness of the Lord in the land of the living.

PSALM 27:8,13 NASB

The minute I said, "I'm slipping, I'm falling,"
your love, God, took hold and held me fast.
When I was upset and beside myself, you
calmed me down and cheered me up.

PSALM 94:18,19 THE MESSAGE

Now to Him who is able to keep you from
stumbling, and to make you stand in the presence of His glory blameless with great joy, to the
only God our Savior, through Jesus Christ our
Lord, be glory, majesty, dominion and authority.

JUDE 24,25 NASB

Q: SOMETIMES I FEEL LIKE NO
ONE CARES. AM I SPECIAL
TO YOU, LORD?

A: Of all the people on earth, the Lord your
God has chosen you to be his own special treasure.... He will love you and bless you.

DEUTERONOMY 7:6,13 NLT

"Before I formed you in the womb I knew
you, before you were born I set you apart."

JEREMIAH 1:5 NIV

He pays...attention to you, down to the last
detail — even numbering the hairs on your
head!

MATTHEW 10:30 THE MESSAGE

You know when I sit down or stand up. You
know my every thought.... You know what I
am going to say even before I say it, Lord....
You made all the delicate, inner parts of my
body and knit me together in my mother's
womb.... You saw me before I was born. Every

day of my life was recorded in your book. Every moment was laid out before a single day had passed. How precious are your thoughts about me, O God! They are innumerable! I can't even count them; they outnumber the grains of sand!

PSALM 139:2,4,13,16,17 NLT

You keep track of all my sorrows. You have collected all my tears in your bottle. You have recorded each one in your book.

PSALM 56:8 NLT

Long ago, even before he made the world, God chose us to be his very own.... His unchanging plan has always been to adopt us into his own family by sending Jesus Christ to die for us. And he did this because he wanted to!

EPHESIANS 1:4,5 TLB

Each of us is an original.

GALATIANS 5:26 THE MESSAGE

We are able to hold our heads high no matter what happens and know that all is well, for we know how dearly God loves us, and we feel this warm love everywhere within us because

God has given us the Holy Spirit to fill our hearts with his love.

ROMANS 5:5 TLB

We know how much God loves us because we have felt his love and because we believe him when he tells us that he loves us dearly.

1 JOHN 4:16 TLB

PROMISES

God promises to love me all day, sing songs all through the night! My life is God's prayer.

PSALM 42:8 THE MESSAGE

When my father and my mother forsake me, then the Lord will take care of me.

PSALM 27:10 NKJV

PRAYERS

May you be able to feel and understand, as all God's children should, how long, how wide, how deep, and how high his love really is; and to experience this love for yourselves, though it is so great that you will never see the end of it or fully know or understand it.

EPHESIANS 3:18,19 TLB

———❖———

Q: LORD, I KNOW YOU CAN HEAL ME, BUT WILL YOU?

———❖———

A: The Lord says, "I will rescue those who love me. I will protect those who trust in my name. When they call on me, I will answer; I will be with them in trouble. I will rescue them and honor them. I will satisfy them with a long life and give them my salvation."

PSALM 91:14-16 NLT

I am the Lord that healeth thee.

EXODUS 15:26 KJV

INSTRUCTIONS

Trust in the Lord with all your heart and do not lean on your own understanding. In all your ways acknowledge Him, and He will make your paths straight. Do not be wise in your own eyes; fear the Lord and turn away from evil. It will be healing to your body and refreshment to your bones. PROVERBS 3:5-8 NASB

Pay attention, my child, to what I say. Listen carefully. Don't lose sight of my words. Let them penetrate deep within your heart, for they bring life and radiant health to anyone who discovers their meaning.

PROVERBS 4:20-22 NLT

Is any one of you sick? He should call the elders of the church to pray over him and anoint him with oil in the name of the Lord. And the prayer offered in faith will make the sick person well; the Lord will raise him up. If he has sinned, he will be forgiven. Therefore confess your sins to each other and pray for each other so that you may be healed. The prayer of a righteous man is powerful and effective.

JAMES 5:14-16 NIV

"These signs will follow those who believe: In My name they will cast out demons...they will lay hands on the sick, and they will recover."

MARK 16:17,18 NKJV

The truth is, anyone who believes in me will do the same works I have done, and even greater works, because I am going to be with the

Father. You can ask for anything in my name, and I will do it, because the work of the Son brings glory to the Father.

JOHN 14:12,13 NLT

Give thanks to the Lord and proclaim his greatness. Let the whole world know what he has done. Sing to him; yes, sing his praises. Tell everyone about his miracles.... O worshipers of the Lord, rejoice!

PSALM 105:1-3 NLT

Never give up praying. And when you pray, keep alert and be thankful.

COLOSSIANS 4:2 CEV

PROMISES

Of all the people on earth, the Lord your God has chosen you to be his own special treasure... He is the faithful God who keeps his covenant for a thousand generations and constantly loves those who love him and obey his commands. He will love you and bless you. And the Lord will protect you from all sickness.

DEUTERONOMY 7:6,9,13,15 NLT

"I will restore you to health and heal your wounds," declares the Lord.

JEREMIAH 30:17 NIV

He took our suffering on him and felt our pain for us. We saw his suffering. We thought God was punishing him. But he was wounded for the wrong things we did. He was crushed for the evil things we did. The punishment, which made us well, was given to him. And we are healed because of his wounds.

ISAIAH 53:4,5 ICB

You must worship the Lord your God. If you do, I will bless your bread and your water. I will take away sickness from you. I will allow you to live long lives.

EXODUS 23:25,26 ICB

Jesus said to him, "I will go and heal him."

MATTHEW 8:7 NIV

He sent forth his word and healed them; he rescued them from the grave.

PSALM 107:20 NIV

PRAYERS

What shall I render to the Lord for all His benefits toward me? I will take up the cup of salvation, and call upon the name of the Lord. I will offer to You the sacrifice of thanksgiving, and will call upon the name of the Lord.

PSALM 116:12,13,17 NKJV

Oh my soul, bless God, don't forget a single
blessing! He forgives your sins — every one.
He heals your diseases — every one.

PSALM 103:2,3 THE MESSAGE

Lord, how you have helped me before! You
took me safely from my mother's womb and
brought me through the years of infancy. I have
depended upon you since birth; you have always
been my God. Don't leave me now, for trouble
is near and no one else can possibly help.

PSALM 22:9-11 TLB

I pray that God, who gives peace, will make
you completely holy. And may your spirit, soul,
and body be kept healthy and faultless until
our Lord Jesus returns. The one who chose you
can be trusted, and he will do this.

1 THESSALONIANS 5:23,24 CEV

He is my God, and I am trusting him. For he
rescues you from every trap, and protects you
from the fatal plague. He will shield you with
his wings! They will shelter you. His faithful

promises are your armor.

PSALM 91:2-4 TLB

"Whatever you ask for in prayer, believe that you have received it, and it will be yours."

MARK 11:24 NIV

EXAMPLES

There are many examples in the Bible of people asking for — and receiving — healing. Here are two:

Two blind men followed him, calling out, "Have mercy on us, Son of David!"... He asked them, "Do you believe that I am able to do this?" "Yes, Lord," they replied. Then he touched their eyes and said, "According to your faith will it be done to you."

MATTHEW 9:27-29 NIV

A man with leprosy came and knelt before him and said, "Lord, if you are willing, you can make me clean." Jesus reached out his hand and touched the man. "I am willing," he said. "Be clean!" Immediately he was cured of his leprosy.

MATTHEW 8:2,3 NIV

Jesus Christ never changes! He is the same yesterday, today, and forever.

HEBREWS 13:8 CEV

---◇◇◇---

Q: LORD, I'VE PRAYED, BUT
NOTHING HAS CHANGED.
WHAT SHOULD I DO?

---◇◇◇---

A: Trust in the Lord, and do good; dwell in
the land, and feed on His faithfulness. Delight
yourself also in the Lord, and He shall give you
the desires of your heart. Commit your way to
the Lord, trust also in Him, and He shall bring
it to pass. Rest in the Lord, and wait patiently
for Him.

PSALM 37:3-5,7 NKJV

INSTRUCTIONS

You need to persevere so that when you have
done the will of God, you will receive what he
has promised.

HEBREWS 10:36 NIV

Therefore, take up the full armor of God, so
that you may be able to resist in the evil day,
and having done everything, to stand firm.

EPHESIANS 6:13 NASB

Wait...for God. Wait with hope. Hope now; hope always!

PSALM 131:3 THE MESSAGE

"Have faith in God," Jesus answered. "I tell you the truth, if anyone says to this mountain, 'Go, throw yourself into the sea,' and does not doubt in his heart but believes that what he says will happen, it will be done for him. Therefore I tell you, whatever you ask for in prayer, believe that you have received it, and it will be yours."

MARK 11:22-24 NIV

Be like those who through faith and patience will receive what God has promised.

HEBREWS 6:12 NCV

Stay with God! Take heart. Don't quit. I'll say it again: Stay with God.

PSALM 27:14 THE MESSAGE

PRAYERS

May the God of hope fill you with all joy and peace as you trust in him, so that you may overflow with hope by the power of the Holy Spirit.

ROMANS 15:13 NIV

We pray that you'll have the strength to stick it out over the long haul — not the grim strength of gritting your teeth but the glory-strength God gives. It is strength that endures the unendurable and spills over into joy.

COLOSSIANS 1:11 THE MESSAGE

PROMISES

Everything that was written in the past was written to teach us. The Scriptures give us patience and encouragement so that we can have hope. Patience and encouragement come from God.

ROMANS 15:4,5 NCV

He gives power to the faint and weary, and to him who has no might He increases strength.

ISAIAH 40:29 AMP

But those who hope in the Lord will renew their strength. They will soar on wings like eagles; they will run and not grow weary, they will walk and not be faint.

ISAIAH 40:31 NIV

Don't worry about anything; instead, pray about everything. Tell God what you need, and thank him for all he has done. If you do this, you will experience God's peace, which is far more wonderful than the human mind can understand. His peace will guard your hearts and minds as you live in Christ Jesus.

PHILIPPIANS 4:6,7 NLT

The earnest (heartfelt, continued) prayer of a righteous man makes tremendous power available — dynamic in its working. JAMES 5:16 AMP

We who have run for our very lives to God have every reason to grab the promised hope with both hands and never let go. It's an unbreakable spiritual lifeline, reaching past all appearances right to the very presence of God.

HEBREWS 6:18,19 THE MESSAGE

We continue to shout our praise even when we're hemmed in with troubles, because we know how troubles can develop passionate patience in us, and how that patience in turn forges the tempered steel of virtue, keeping us alert for whatever God will do next.

ROMANS 5:3,4 THE MESSAGE

EXAMPLE

Abraham kept believing God's promise to him, no matter what he saw or felt:

There was no hope that Abraham would have children. But Abraham believed God and continued hoping, and so he became the father of many nations. As God told him, "Your descendants also will be too many to count." Abraham was almost a hundred years old, much past the age for having children, and Sarah could not have children. Abraham thought about all this, but his faith in God did not become weak. He never doubted that God would keep his promise, and he never stopped believing. He grew stronger in his faith and gave praise to God. Abraham felt sure that God was able to do what he had promised.

ROMANS 4:18-21 NCV

And so after waiting patiently, Abraham received what was promised.
HEBREWS 6:15 NIV

—◇◇◇—

Q: LORD, I'M HAVING MONEY
TROUBLE. DO YOU
HAVE ANY ADVICE FOR ME?

—◇◇◇—

A: "I am the Lord your God, who teaches you to profit, who leads you in the way you should go."

ISAIAH 48:17 NASB

The reward of humility and the fear of the Lord are riches, honor and life.

PROVERBS 22:4 NASB

INSTRUCTIONS

In everything you do, put God first, and he will direct you and crown your efforts with success.

PROVERBS 3:6 TLB

For the Lord gives wisdom; from His mouth come knowledge and understanding

PROVERBS 2:6-8 NKJV

The Lord will guide you continually.

ISAIAH 58:11 NKJV

LORD, I'M HAVING MONEY TROUBLE.
DO YOU HAVE ANY ADVICE?

"Your heavenly Father already knows all your needs, and he will give you all you need from day to day if you live for him and make the Kingdom of God your primary concern. So don't worry about tomorrow, for tomorrow will bring its own worries. Today's trouble is enough for today."

MATTHEW 6:32-34 NLT

Lazy hands make a man poor, but diligent hands bring wealth.

PROVERBS 10:4 NIV

The sluggard craves and gets nothing, but the desires of the diligent are fully satisfied.

PROVERBS 13:4 NIV

Lust for money brings trouble and nothing but trouble. Going down that path, some lose their footing in the faith completely and live to regret it bitterly ever after.

1 TIMOTHY 6:10 THE MESSAGE

Don't be obsessed with getting more material things.

HEBREWS 13:5 THE MESSAGE

Keep your lives free from the love of money, and be satisfied with what you have.

HEBREWS 13:5 NCV

"You can't worship two gods at once. Loving one god, you'll end up hating the other. Adoration of one feeds contempt for the other. You can't worship God and Money both."

MATTHEW 6:24 THE MESSAGE

"Bring all the tithes into the storehouse so there will be enough food in my Temple. If you do," says the Lord Almighty, "I will open the windows of heaven for you. I will pour out a blessing so great you won't have enough room to take it in! Try it! Let me prove it to you!"

MALACHI 3:10 NLT

PROMISES

For if you give, you will get! Your gift will return to you in full and overflowing measure, pressed down, shaken together to make room for more, and running over. Whatever measure you use to give — large or small — will be used to measure what is given back to you.

LUKE 6:38 TLB

Those who seek the Lord shall not lack any good thing.

PSALM 34:10 NKJV

The blessing of the Lord makes one rich, and He adds no sorrow with it.

PROVERBS 10:22 NKJV

This same God who takes care of me will supply all your needs from his glorious riches, which have been given to us in Christ Jesus.

PHILIPPIANS 4:19 NLT

PRAYERS

"The Lord be magnified, who delights in the prosperity of His servant."

PSALM 35:27 NASB

"Both riches and honor come from You, and You rule over all, and in Your hand is power and might; and it lies in Your hand to make great and to strengthen everyone."

1 CHRONICLES 29:12 NASB

Though I walk in the midst of trouble, you preserve my life.... The Lord will fulfill his purpose for me.

PSALM 138:7,8 NIV

Q: IT'S HARD TO ALWAYS
TELL THE TRUTH, LORD. HOW
CAN I QUIT LYING?

A: Lovingly follow the truth at all times —
speaking truly, dealing truly, living truly — and
so become more and more in every way like
Christ.

EPHESIANS 4:15 TLB

INSTRUCTIONS

Be an example...with your words, your actions,
your love, your faith, and your pure life.

1 TIMOTHY 4:12 NCV

Tell your neighbor the truth....When you lie to
others, you end up lying to yourself.

EPHESIANS 4:25 THE MESSAGE

An honest life shows respect for God; a
degenerate life is a slap in his face.

PROVERBS 14:2 THE MESSAGE

Stop lying to each other. You have given up your old way of life with its habits. Each of you is now a new person. You are becoming more and more like your Creator.

COLOSSIANS 3:9,10 CEV

The person who tells lies gets caught; the person who spreads rumors is ruined.

PROVERBS 19:9 THE MESSAGE

These liars have lied so well and for so long that they've lost their capacity for truth.

1 TIMOTHY 4:2 THE MESSAGE

PROMISES

Do any of you want to live a life that is long and good? Then watch your tongue! Keep your lips from telling lies! Turn away from evil and do good.... The Lord hears his people when they call to him for help. He rescues them from all their troubles...from each and every one.

PSALM 34:12-14,17,19 NLT

If anyone is in Christ, he is a new creation; old

things have passed away; behold, all things have become new.

2 CORINTHIANS 5:17 NKJV

God is working in you to make you willing and able to obey him.

PHILIPPIANS 2:13 CEV

PRAYERS

You deserve honesty from the heart; yes, utter sincerity and truthfulness.... Create in me a new, clean heart, O God, filled with clean thoughts and right desires.

PSALM 51:6,10 TLB

You want me to be completely truthful. So teach me wisdom. Take away my sin, and I will be clean. Wash me, and I will be whiter than snow.

PSALM 51:6,7 ICB

We pray that you will also have great wisdom and understanding in spiritual things so that you will live the kind of life that honors and pleases the Lord in every way.... God has freed us from the power of darkness, and he brought us into the kingdom of his dear Son.

COLOSSIANS 1:9,10,13 NCV

EXAMPLES

There are many accounts in the Bible of people lying. Notice how both of these lies brought consequences:

Then Peter began to curse. He said, "May a curse fall on me if I'm not telling the truth. I don't know the man." After Peter said this, a rooster crowed. Then he remembered what Jesus had told him: "Before the rooster crows, you will say three times that you don't know me." Then Peter went outside and cried painfully.

MATTHEW 26:74,75 ICB

Elisha said to him, "Where did you go, Gehazi?" And he said, "Your servant did not go anywhere." Then he said to him, "Did not my heart go with you when the man turned back from his chariot to meet you? Is it time to receive money and to receive clothing, olive groves and vineyards, sheep and oxen, male and female servants? Therefore the leprosy of Naaman shall cling to you and your descendants forever." And he went out from his presence leprous, as white as snow.

2 KINGS 5:25-27 NKJV

—◇—

Q: LORD, WHAT IF SOMEONE MAKES FUN OF ME BECAUSE I BELIEVE IN YOU?

—◇—

A: Fear not, for I am with you; be not dismayed, for I am your God. I will strengthen you, yes, I will help you, I will uphold you with My righteous right hand. Behold, all those who were incensed against you shall be ashamed and disgraced.

ISAIAH 41:10,11 NKJV

For the Lord God helps me...therefore have I set my face like a flint, and I know that I shall not be put to shame.

ISAIAH 50:7 AMP

INSTRUCTIONS

Be an example to the believers with your words, your actions, your love, your faith, and your pure life.

1 TIMOTHY 4:12 NCV

You're blessed when your commitment to God

provokes persecution. The persecution drives you even deeper into God's kingdom. "Not only that — count yourselves blessed every time people put you down or throw you out or speak lies about you to discredit me. What it means is that the truth is too close for comfort and they are uncomfortable. You can be glad when that happens — give a cheer, even! — for though they don't like it, I do! And all heaven applauds. And know that you are in good company. My prophets and witnesses have always gotten into this kind of trouble."

MATTHEW 5:10-12 THE MESSAGE

For I am not ashamed of the gospel of Christ, for it is the power of God to salvation for everyone who believes.

ROMANS 1:16 NKJV

We work hard and suffer much in order that people will believe the truth, for our hope is in the living God, who is the Savior of all people.

1 TIMOTHY 4:10 NLT

Stay away from foolish and stupid arguments, because you know they grow into quarrels. And a servant of the Lord must not quarrel but must be kind to everyone, a good teacher, and patient. The Lord's servant must gently teach those who disagree.

2 TIMOTHY 2:23-25 NCV

If someone mistreats you because you are a Christian, don't curse him; pray that God will bless him.

ROMANS 12:14 TLB

Put on the full armor of God, so that when the day of evil comes, you may be able to stand your ground.

EPHESIANS 6:13 NIV

PROMISES

The good man does not escape all troubles — he has them too. But the Lord helps him in each and every one.

PSALM 34:19 TLB

You are of God, little children, and have overcome them, because He who is in you is greater than he who is in the world.

1 JOHN 4:4 NKJV

Fear of man will prove to be a snare, but whoever trusts in the Lord is kept safe.

PROVERBS 29:25 NIV

He Himself has said, "I will never leave you nor forsake you." So we may boldly say: "The

Lord is my helper; I will not fear. What can man do to me?"

HEBREWS 13:5,6 NKJV

I give you peace, the kind of peace that only I can give. It isn't like the peace that this world can give. So don't be worried or afraid.

JOHN 14:27 CEV

PRAYERS

Lord, defend me. I have lived an innocent life. I trusted the Lord and never doubted. Lord, try me and test me. Look closely into my heart and mind. I see your love. I live by your truth. I do not spend time with liars. I do not make friends with people who hide their sin. I hate the company of evil people.... I have lived an innocent life. So save me and be kind to me.

PSALM 26:1-5,11 ICB

The Lord is my light and my salvation; whom shall I fear? The Lord is the strength of my life; of whom shall I be afraid?

PSALM 27:1 NKJV

If God is for us, who can be against us?

ROMANS 8:31 NKJV

May the God of peace himself make you entirely pure and devoted to God; and may your spirit and soul and body be kept strong and blameless until that day when our Lord Jesus Christ comes back again.

1 THESSALONIANS 5:23 TLB

EXAMPLES

Shadrach, Meshach, and Abednego stood together against tremendous pressure. Because they steadfastly refused to bow down and worship the golden idol, God protected and promoted them:

The fire hadn't touched them — not a hair of their heads was singed; their coats were unscorched, and they didn't even smell of smoke! Then Nebuchadnezzar said, "Blessed be the God of Shadrach, Meshach, and Abednego, for he sent his angel to deliver his trusting servants when they defied the king's commandment, and were willing to die rather than serve or worship any god except their own." Then the king gave promotions to Shadrach, Meshach, and Abednego, so that they prospered greatly there in the province of Babylon.

DANIEL 3:27,28,30 TLB

—◆—

Q: I HAVE TOO MUCH TO DO.
HOW CAN I COPE WITH
ALL THIS STRESS?

—◆—

A: "Do not let your hearts be troubled.
Trust in God; trust also in me.... Peace I leave
with you; my peace I give you. I do not give to
you as the world gives. Do not...be afraid."

JOHN 14:1,27 NIV

Don't fret or worry. Instead of worrying, pray.
Let petitions and praises shape your worries
into prayers, letting God know your concerns.
Before you know it, a sense of God's wholeness, everything coming together for good, will
come and settle you down. It's wonderful what
happens when Christ displaces worry at the
center of your life.

PHILIPPIANS 4:6-8 THE MESSAGE

INSTRUCTIONS

Pile your troubles on God's shoulders — he'll

carry your load, he'll help you out.

PSALM 55:22 THE MESSAGE

"Give your entire attention to what God is doing right now, and don't get worked up about what may or may not happen tomorrow. God will help you deal with whatever hard things come up when the time comes."

MATTHEW 6:34 THE MESSAGE

PROMISES

A thousand may fall at your side, ten thousand at your right hand, but it will not come near you.... If you make the Most High your dwelling — even the Lord, who is my refuge — then no harm will befall you, no disaster will come near your tent.

PSALM 91:7,9,10 NIV

No temptation has seized you except what is common to man. And God is faithful; he will not let you be tempted beyond what you can bear. But when you are tempted, he will also provide a way out so that you can stand up under it.

1 CORINTHIANS 10:13 NIV

How blessed the man you train, God, the woman you instruct in your Word, providing a circle of quiet within the clamor of evil.

PSALM 94:12,13 THE MESSAGE

In the multitude of my anxieties within me, Your comforts delight my soul.

PSALM 94:19 NKJV

I can do all things through Christ who strengthens me.

PHILIPPIANS 4:13 NKJV

If you need wisdom — if you want to know what God wants you to do — ask him, and he will gladly tell you.

JAMES 1:5 NLT

Wisdom and truth will enter the very center of your being, filling your life with joy.

PROVERBS 2:10 TLB

PRAYERS

The minute I said, "I'm slipping, I'm falling," your love, God, took hold and held me fast. When I was upset and beside myself, you calmed me down and cheered me up.

PSALM 94:18,19 THE MESSAGE

You are my hiding place! You protect me from trouble, and you put songs in my heart because you have saved me.

PSALM 32:7 CEV

Teach me wisdom.

PSALM 51:6 ICB

EXAMPLE

We can trust God to give us wisdom. When Moses was overwhelmed with the responsibility of caring for the nation of Israel, God provided a plan that took the pressure off:

"What you are doing is not good. You and these people who come to you will only wear yourselves out. The work is too heavy for you; you cannot handle it alone.... But select capable men from all the people...and appoint them as officials over thousands, hundreds, fifties and tens. That will make your load lighter, because they will share it with you."

EXODUS 18:17,18,21,22 NIV

---❖---

Q: LORD, EVERYTHING SEEMS
SO HOPELESS — I WISH I
COULD DIE. HOW CAN I
GO ON?

---❖---

A: "For I know the plans that I have for you," declares the Lord, "plans for welfare and not for calamity to give you a future and a hope.... You will seek Me and find Me when you search for Me with all your heart. I will be found by you...and I will restore your fortunes."

JEREMIAH 29:11,13,14 NASB

Surely there is a future, and your hope will not be cut off.

PROVERBS 23:18 NASB

PRAYERS

You have searched me and known me. You know my sitting down and my rising up; You understand my thought afar off. You comprehend my path and my lying down, and are acquainted with all my ways. For there is not a word on my tongue, but behold, O Lord, You know it altogether.... Such knowledge is too wonderful for me; it is high, I cannot attain it.

Where can I go from Your Spirit? Or where can I flee from Your presence? If I ascend into heaven, You are there; if I make my bed in hell, behold, You are there. If I take the wings of the morning, and dwell in the uttermost parts of the sea, even there Your hand shall lead me, and Your right hand shall hold me.

How precious also are Your thoughts to me, O God! How great is the sum of them! If I should count them, they would be more in number than the sand; when I awake, I am still with You.... Lead me in the way everlasting.

PSALM 139:1-4,6-10,17,18,24 NKJV

Whom have I in heaven but you? And earth has nothing I desire besides you. My flesh and my heart may fail, but God is the strength of my heart and my portion forever.... It is good to be near God. I have made the Sovereign Lord my refuge.

PSALM 73:25,26,28 NIV

Though I walk in the midst of trouble, You will revive me; You will stretch out Your hand against the wrath of my enemies, and Your right hand will save me. The Lord will perfect that which concerns me; Your mercy, O Lord, endures forever.

PSALM 138:7,8 NKJV

The Lord will fulfil his purpose for me; your love, O Lord, endures forever.

PSALM 138:8 NIV

He Himself has said, "I will never leave you nor forsake you." So we may boldly say: "The Lord is my helper; I will not fear. What can man do to me?"

HEBREWS 13:5,6 NKJV

I am leaving you with a gift — peace of mind and heart! And the peace I give isn't fragile like the peace the world gives. So don't be troubled or afraid.

JOHN 14:27 TLB

May the God of hope fill you with all joy and peace as you trust in him, so that you may overflow with hope by the power of the Holy Spirit.

ROMANS 15:13 NIV

EXAMPLE

In the face of all his suffering, Job wanted to die. He felt like God and the universe were against him.

Oh, that I might have my request, and that God would grant me the thing that I long for! I even wish that it would please God to crush me; that He would let loose His hand and cut me off!.... What strength have I left, that I should wait and hope? And what is ahead of me, that I should be patient?

JOB 6:8,9,11 AMP

Fortunately, Job didn't give up too soon, since God had great plans for his future. God revealed Himself to Job, then doubled his wealth and happiness.

I have heard of You [only] by the hearing of the ear; but now my [spiritual] eye sees You.

JOB 42:5 AMP

The Lord blessed Job at the end of his life more than at the beginning.... Job lived 140 years after that, living to see his grandchildren and great-grandchildren too. Then at last he died, an old, old man, after living a long, good life.

JOB 42:12,16,17 TLB

Q: I believe in God and I go to church. Is that enough... or is there more?

A: He...said, Men, what is it necessary for me to do that I may be saved?

And they answered, Believe in and on the Lord Jesus Christ — that is, give yourself up to Him, take yourself out of your own keeping and entrust yourself into His keeping, and you will be saved.   Acts 16:30,31 AMP

Jesus replied, "I assure you, unless you are born again, you can never see the Kingdom of God."

"What do you mean?" exclaimed Nicodemus. "How can an old man go back into his mother's womb and be born again?"

Jesus replied, "The truth is, no one can enter the Kingdom of God without being born of water and the Spirit. Humans can reproduce only human life, but the Holy Spirit gives new life from heaven."   John 3:3-6 NLT

For God so greatly loved and dearly prized the world that He [even] gave up His only-begotten (unique) Son, so that whoever believes in (trusts, clings to, relies on) Him shall not perish — come to destruction, be lost — but have eternal (everlasting) life.

JOHN 3:16 AMP

Anyone who trusts in him is acquitted; anyone who refuses to trust him has long since been under the death sentence without knowing it. And why? Because of that person's failure to believe in the one-of-a-kind Son of God when introduced to him.

JOHN 3:18 THE MESSAGE

And all who trust him — God's Son — to save them have eternal life.

JOHN 3:36 TLB

For if you do not believe that I am He [Who I claim to be] — if you do not adhere to, trust in and rely on Me — you will die in your sins.

JOHN 8:24 AMP

Q: JESUS, I WANT TO BELIEVE IN
YOU. HOW CAN I BE SURE YOU
ARE REALLY REAL?

A: You will seek Me, inquire for and require
Me [as a vital necessity] and find Me; when
you search for Me with all your heart, I will be
found by you, says the Lord.

JEREMIAH 29:13,14 AMP

"For everyone who asks receives, and he who
seeks finds, and to him who knocks it will be
opened."
MATTHEW 7:8 NASB

All who seek the Lord will praise him. Their
hearts will rejoice with everlasting joy.

PSALM 22:26 NLT

The person who has My commands and keeps
them is the one who [really] loves Me, and
whoever [really] loves Me will be loved by My
Father. And I [too] will love him and will
show (reveal, manifest) Myself to him — I will

let Myself be clearly seen by him and make
Myself real to him.

JOHN 14:21 AMP

INSTRUCTIONS

Before you trust, you have to listen. But unless
Christ's Word is preached, there's nothing to
listen to.

ROMANS 10:17 THE MESSAGE

For what I received I passed on to you as of
first importance: that Christ died for our sins
according to the Scriptures, that he was buried,
that he was raised on the third day according
to the Scriptures, and that he appeared to
Peter, and then to the Twelve. After that, he
appeared to more than five hundred of the
brothers at the same time

1 CORINTHIANS 15:3-6 NIV

To these He also presented Himself alive after
His suffering, by many convincing proofs,
appearing to them over a period of forty days
and speaking of the things concerning the
kingdom of God.

ACTS 1:3 NASB

There are also many other things that Jesus
did, which if they were written one by one, I

suppose that even the world itself could not contain the books that would be written.

JOHN 21:25 NKJV

These have been written so that you may believe that Jesus is the Christ, the Son of God; and that believing you may have life in His name.

JOHN 20:31 NASB

For you know that God paid a ransom to save you from the empty life you inherited from your ancestors. And the ransom he paid was not mere gold or silver. He paid for you with the precious lifeblood of Christ, the sinless, spotless Lamb of God. God chose him for this purpose long before the world began, but now in these final days, he was sent to the earth for all to see. And he did this for you.

Through Christ you have come to trust in God. And because God raised Christ from the dead and gave him great glory, your faith and hope can be placed confidently in God.

For you have been born again. Your new life did not come from your earthly parents because the life they gave you will end in death. But this new life will last forever

because it comes from the eternal, living word
of God.

1 PETER 1:18-21,23 NLT

Can you imagine the breathtaking recovery
life makes, sovereign life, in those who grasp
with both hands this wildly extravagant life-
gift, this grand setting-everything-right, that
the one man Jesus Christ provides? Here it is
in a nutshell: Just as one person [Adam] did it
wrong and got us in all this trouble with sin
and death, another person did it right and got
us out of it. But more than just getting us out
of trouble, he got us into life!

ROMANS 5:17,18 THE MESSAGE

PROMISES

He is real and...he rewards those who truly
want to find him.

HEBREWS 11:6 NCV

"No one's ever seen or heard anything like
this, never so much as imagined anything quite
like it — what God has arranged for those
who love him." But you've seen and heard it
because God by his Spirit has brought it all out
into the open before you.

We didn't learn this by reading books or going to school; we learned it from God, who taught us person-to-person through Jesus, and we're passing it on to you in the same first-hand, personal way.

The unspiritual self, just as it is by nature, can't receive the gifts of God's Spirit. There's no capacity for them. They seem like so much silliness. Spirit can be known only by spirit — God's Spirit and our spirits in open communion.

1 CORINTHIANS 2:9,13-15 THE MESSAGE

God once said, "Let the light shine out of the darkness!" This is the same God who made his light shine in our hearts by letting us know the glory of God that is in the face of Christ.

2 CORINTHIANS 4:6 NCV

PRAYERS

I pray for you constantly, asking God, the glorious Father of our Lord Jesus Christ, to give you wisdom to see clearly and really understand who Christ is and all that he has done for you. I pray that your hearts will be flooded with light so that you can see something of the future he has called you to share.... I pray that you will begin to understand how incredibly great his power is to help those who believe him.

EPHESIANS 1:17-19 TLB

Hear my voice when I call, O Lord; be merciful to me and answer me. My heart says of you, "Seek his face!" Your face, Lord, I will seek.

PSALM 27:7,8 NIV

EXAMPLE

"Doubting Thomas" said he had to see for himself that Jesus was alive (John 20:24,25). Jesus appeared to him and said:

"Put your finger here; see my hands. Reach out your hand and put it into my side. Stop doubting and believe." Thomas said to him, "My Lord and my God!"

JOHN 20:27,28 NIV

Jesus said, "So, you believe because you've seen with your own eyes. Even better blessings are in store for those who believe without seeing."

JOHN 20:29 THE MESSAGE

Q: Is there something
I need to do to begin
a relationship with You,
Lord? How do I
get started?

A: Salvation that comes from trusting
Christ...is already within easy reach. In fact,
the Scriptures say, "The message is close at
hand; it is on your lips and in your heart."
For if you confess with your mouth that Jesus
is Lord and believe in your heart that God
raised him from the dead, you will be saved.
For it is by believing in your heart that you are
made right with God, and it is by confessing
with your mouth that you are saved. As the
Scriptures tell us, "Anyone who believes in him
will not be disappointed."   ROMANS 10:8-11 NLT

"The word that saves is right here, as near as
the tongue in your mouth, as close as the
heart in your chest." It's the word of faith that

welcomes God to go to work and set things right for us.

ROMANS 10:8 THE MESSAGE

PROMISES

To all who believed him and accepted him, he gave the right to become children of God. They are reborn! This is not a physical birth resulting from human passion or plan — this rebirth comes from God.

JOHN 1:12,13 NLT

Therefore, if anyone is in Christ, he is a new creation; old things have passed away; behold, all things have become new.

2 CORINTHIANS 5:17 NKJV

God our Savior showed us how good and kind he is. He saved us because of his mercy, and not because of any good things that we have done. God washed us by the power of the Holy Spirit. He gave us new birth and a fresh beginning. God sent Jesus Christ our Savior to give us his Spirit. Jesus treated us much better than we deserve. He made us acceptable to God and gave us the hope of eternal life.

TITUS 3:4-7 CEV

If we say we have fellowship with God, but we continue living in darkness, we are liars and do not follow the truth. But if we live in the light, as God is in the light, we can share fellowship with each other. Then the blood of Jesus, God's Son, cleanses us from every sin.

If we say we have no sin, we are fooling ourselves, and the truth is not in us. But if we confess our sins, he will forgive our sins, because we can trust God to do what is right. He will cleanse us from all the wrongs we have done.

1 JOHN 1:6-9 NCV

PRAYERS

Say the welcoming word to God — "Jesus is my Master" — embracing, body and soul, God's work of doing in us what he did in raising Jesus from the dead. That's it. You're not "doing" anything; you're simply calling out to God, trusting him to do it for you. That's salvation. With your whole being you embrace God setting things right, and then you say it, right out loud: "God has set everything right between him and me!"

ROMANS 10:9,10 THE MESSAGE

———❈———

Q: GOD, THE BIBLE CALLS YOU OUR FATHER IN HEAVEN. HOW ARE YOU LIKE A FATHER TO ME?

———❈———

A: He surrounds me with lovingkindness and tender mercies. He fills my life with good things!

PSALM 103:4,5 TLB

The Lord is merciful and gracious; he is slow to get angry and full of unfailing love. He will not constantly accuse us, nor remain angry forever. He has not punished us for all our sins, nor does he deal with us as we deserve. For his unfailing love toward those who fear him is as great as the height of the heavens above the earth. He has removed our rebellious acts as far away from us as the east is from the west.

The Lord is like a father to his children, tender and compassionate to those who fear him. For he understands how weak we are; he knows we are only dust.

PSALM 103:8-14 NLT

Whatever is good and perfect comes to us from God above, who created all heaven's lights. Unlike them, he never changes or casts shifting shadows. In his goodness he chose to make us his own children by giving us his true word. And we, out of all creation, became his choice possession.

JAMES 1:17,18 NLT

If God gives such attention to the appearance of wildflowers — most of which are never even seen — don't you think he'll attend to you, take pride in you, do his best for you?

MATTHEW 6:30 THE MESSAGE

I will instruct you and teach you in the way which you should go; I will counsel you with My eye upon you.

PSALM 32:8 NASB

Your ears shall hear a word behind you, saying, "This is the way, walk in it," whenever you turn to the right hand or whenever you turn to the left.

ISAIAH 30:21 NKJV

"The Lord corrects the people he loves and disciplines those he calls his own."

HEBREWS 12:6 CEV

The Father is a merciful God, who always gives us comfort. He comforts us when we are in trouble, so that we can share that same comfort with others in trouble.

2 CORINTHIANS 1:3,4 CEV

And we have known and believed the love that God has for us. God is love. We love Him because He first loved us.

1 JOHN 4:16,19 NKJV

We used to be stupid, disobedient, and foolish, as well as slaves of all sorts of desires and pleasures. We were evil and jealous. Everyone hated us, and we hated everyone. God our Savior showed us how good and kind he is. He saved us because of his mercy, and not because of any good things that we have done. God washed us by the power of the Holy Spirit. He gave us new birth and a fresh beginning. God sent Jesus Christ our Savior to give us his Spirit.

TITUS 3:3-6 CEV

It was all his doing; we had nothing to do with it. He gave us a good bath, and we came out of it new people, washed inside and out by the Holy Spirit.

TITUS 3:4-7 THE MESSAGE

PROMISES

"For the eyes of the Lord run to and fro throughout the whole earth, to show Himself strong on behalf of those whose heart is loyal to Him."

2 CHRONICLES 16:9 NKJV

He is a rewarder of those who diligently seek Him.

HEBREWS 11:6 NKJV

The Lord is faithful, and He will strengthen and protect you from the evil one.

2 THESSALONIANS 3:3 NASB

"As a mother comforts her child, so will I comfort you."

ISAIAH 66:13 NIV

And therefore the Lord [earnestly] waits — expectant, looking and longing — to be gracious to you, and therefore He lifts Himself up that He may have mercy on you and show loving-kindness to you...Blessed — happy, fortunate [to be envied] are all those who [earnestly] wait for Him, who expect and look and long for Him [for His victory, His favor, His love, His peace, His joy and His matchless, unbroken companionship].... He will surely be gracious to you at the sound of your cry; when He hears it, He will answer you.

ISAIAH 30:18,19 AMP

"Can a mother forget the baby at her breast and have no compassion on the child she has borne? Though she may forget, I will not forget you! See, I have engraved you on the palms of my hands."

ISAIAH 49:15,16 NIV

"They will be mine," says the Lord Almighty, "in the day when I make up my treasured possession. I will spare them, just as in compassion a man spares his son who serves him."

MALACHI 3:17 NIV

"The Lord your God in your midst, The Mighty One, will save; He will rejoice over you with gladness, He will quiet you with His love, He will rejoice over you with singing."

ZEPHANIAH 3:17 NKJV

The Lord is gracious and compassionate, slow to anger and rich in love. The Lord is good to all; he has compassion on all he has made.

PSALM 145:8,9 NIV

—◊—

Q: I KNOW ABOUT GOD THE
FATHER AND HAVE RECEIVED
JESUS AS MY SAVIOR. WHAT'S THE
HOLY SPIRIT'S ROLE IN MY LIFE?

—◊—

A: I will give you a new heart and put a
new spirit in you; I will remove from you your
heart of stone and give you a heart of flesh.
And I will put my Spirit in you and move you
to follow my decrees and be careful to keep my
laws.
                              EZEKIEL 36:26,27 NIV

INSTRUCTIONS

He washed away our sins and gave us a new
life through the Holy Spirit. He generously
poured out the Spirit upon us because of what
Jesus Christ our Savior did.
                              TITUS 3:5,6 NLT

The name of our Lord Jesus Christ and the
power of God's Spirit have washed you and

made you holy and acceptable to God.

1 CORINTHIANS 6:11 CEV

The power of the life-giving Spirit has freed you through Christ Jesus from the power of sin that leads to death.

ROMANS 8:2 NLT

When I think of the wisdom and scope of God's plan, I fall to my knees and pray to the Father, the Creator of everything in heaven and on earth. I pray that from his glorious, unlimited resources he will give you mighty inner strength through his Holy Spirit.

EPHESIANS 3:14-16 NLT

You should behave...like God's very own children, adopted into his family — calling him "Father, dear Father." For his Holy Spirit speaks to us deep in our hearts and tells us that we are God's children. And since we are his children, we will share his treasures — for everything God gives to his Son, Christ, is ours, too.

ROMANS 8:15-17 NLT

When the Holy Spirit controls our lives, he will produce this kind of fruit in us: love, joy, peace, patience, kindness, goodness, faithfulness, gentleness, and self-control.

GALATIANS 5:22,23 NLT

The Friend, the Holy Spirit whom the Father will send at my request, will make everything plain to you. He will remind you of all the things I have told you.

JOHN 14:26 THE MESSAGE

Jesus said to his disciples: If you love me, you will do as I command. Then I will ask the Father to send you the Holy Spirit who will help you and always be with you. The Spirit will show you what is true. The people of this world cannot accept the Spirit, because they don't see or know him. But you know the Spirit, who is with you and will keep on living in you.

JOHN 14:15-17 CEV

The Spirit shows what is true and will come and guide you into the full truth. The Spirit doesn't speak on his own. He will tell you only what he has heard from me, and he will let you know what is going to happen.

JOHN 16:13 CEV

When the Comforter (Counselor, Helper, Advocate, Intercessor, Strengthener) comes

Whom I will send to you from the Father, the Spirit of Truth Who comes (proceeds) from the Father, He [Himself] will testify regarding Me.

JOHN 15:26 AMP

As it is written in the Scriptures: "No one has ever seen this, and no one has ever heard about it. No one has ever imagined what God has prepared for those who love him." But God has shown us these things through the Spirit.

The Spirit searches out all things, even the deep secrets of God. Who knows the thoughts that another person has? Only a person's spirit that lives within him knows his thoughts. It is the same with God. No one knows the thoughts of God except the Spirit of God. Now we did not receive the spirit of the world, but we received the Spirit that is from God so that we can know all that God has given us.

1 CORINTHIANS 2:9-12 NCV

Those who trust God's action in them find that God's Spirit is in them — living and breathing God!

ROMANS 8:5 THE MESSAGE

The Holy Spirit helps us in our distress. For we don't even know what we should pray for, nor how we should pray. But the Holy Spirit prays for us with groanings that cannot be expressed in words. And the Father who knows all hearts knows what the Spirit is saying, for the Spirit pleads for us believers in harmony with God's own will.

ROMANS 8:26,27 NLT

Dear friends, use your most holy faith to build yourselves up, praying in the Holy Spirit.

JUDE 20 NCV

Pray in the Spirit at all times with all kinds of prayers, asking for everything you need.

EPHESIANS 6:18 NCV

On the final and climactic day of the Feast, Jesus took his stand. He cried out, "If anyone thirsts, let him come to me and drink. Rivers of living water will brim and spill out of the depths of anyone who believes in me this way, just as the Scripture says." (He said this in regard to the Spirit, whom those who believed in him were about to receive. The Spirit had not yet been given because Jesus had not yet been glorified.)

JOHN 7:37-39 THE MESSAGE

He gave them this command: "Do not leave

Jerusalem, but wait for the gift my Father promised, which you have heard me speak about. For John baptized with water, but in a few days you will be baptized with the Holy Spirit."

ACTS 1:4,5 NIV

"You will receive power when the Holy Spirit comes on you; and you will be my witnesses in Jerusalem, and in all Judea and Samaria, and to the ends of the earth."

ACTS 1:8 NIV

And everyone present was filled with the Holy Spirit and began speaking in languages they didn't know, for the Holy Spirit gave them this ability.

ACTS 2:4 TLB

Then Peter stepped forward with the eleven other apostles and shouted to the crowd... "What you see this morning was predicted centuries ago by the prophet Joel:

'In the last days, God said, I will pour out my Spirit upon all people. Your sons and your daughters will prophesy, your young men will see visions, and your old men will dream dreams. In those days I will pour out my Spirit upon all my servants, men and women alike, and they will prophesy.'" ACTS 2:14,16-18 NLT

"Jesus was lifted up to heaven and is now at God's right side. The Father has given the Holy Spirit to Jesus as he promised. So Jesus has poured out that Spirit, and this is what you now see and hear."

ACTS 2:33 NCV

Peter said to them, "Change your hearts and lives and be baptized, each one of you, in the name of Jesus Christ for the forgiveness of your sins. And you will receive the gift of the Holy Spirit. This promise is for you, for your children, and for all who are far away. It is for everyone the Lord our God calls to himself."

ACTS 2:38,39 NCV

While Peter was still speaking these words, the Holy Spirit came on all who heard the message. The circumcised believers who had come with Peter were astonished that the gift of the Holy Spirit had been poured out even on the Gentiles. For they heard them speaking in tongues and praising God. Then Peter said, "Can anyone keep these people from being baptized with water? They have received the

Holy Spirit just as we have." ACTS 10:44-47 NIV

When Paul placed his hands on them, the Holy Spirit came on them, and they spoke in tongues and prophesied. ACTS 19:6 NIV

Don't be drunk with wine, because that will ruin your life. Instead, let the Holy Spirit fill and control you. Then you will sing psalms and hymns and spiritual songs among yourselves, making music to the Lord in your hearts. And you will always give thanks for everything to God the Father in the name of our Lord Jesus Christ. EPHESIANS 5:18-20 NLT

Q: HOW CAN I
PLEASE YOU, GOD?

A: Then one of the scribes...asked Him, "Which is the first commandment of all?"

Jesus answered him, "The first of all the commandments is: 'Hear, O Israel, the Lord our God, the Lord is one. And you shall love the Lord your God with all your heart, with all your soul, with all your mind, and with all your strength.' This is the first commandment. And the second, like it, is this: 'You shall love your neighbor as yourself.' There is no other commandment greater than these."

MARK 12:28-31 NKJV

The Lord delights in those who fear him, who put their hope in his unfailing love.

PSALM 147:11 NIV

"God is Spirit, and those who worship Him must worship in spirit and truth."

JOHN 4:24 NKJV

"That's the kind of people the Father is out looking for: those who are simply and honestly themselves before him in their worship...Those who worship him must do it out of their very being, their spirits, their true selves, in adoration."

JOHN 4:23,24 THE MESSAGE

INSTRUCTIONS

Give unto the Lord the glory due to His name; worship the Lord in the beauty of holiness.

PSALM 29:2 NKJV

Rejoice always, pray without ceasing, in everything give thanks; for this is the will of God in Christ Jesus for you.

1 THESSALONIANS 5:16-18 NKJV

Sing, sing your hearts out to God! Let every detail in your lives — words, actions, whatever — be done in the name of the Master, Jesus, thanking God the Father every step of the way.

COLOSSIANS 3:17 THE MESSAGE

Celebrate God all day, every day. I mean, revel

in him! Don't fret or worry. Instead of worrying, pray. Let petitions and praises shape your worries into prayers, letting God know your concerns. Before you know it, a sense of God's wholeness, everything coming together for good, will come and settle you down. It's wonderful what happens when Christ displaces worry at the center of your life.

PHILIPPIANS 4:4,6,7 THE MESSAGE

Trust in Him at all times, O people; pour out your heart before Him; God is a refuge for us. Selah.

PSALM 62:8 NASB

Fix these words of mine in your hearts and minds...Teach them to your children, talking about them when you sit at home and when you walk along the road, when you lie down and when you get up.

DEUTERONOMY 11:18,19 NIV

Every part of Scripture is God-breathed and useful one way or another — showing us truth, exposing our rebellion, correcting our mistakes, training us to live God's way.

2 TIMOTHY 3:16 THE MESSAGE

PRAYERS

May God, who puts all things together, makes all things whole...Now put you together, provide you with everything you need to please him, make us into what gives him most pleasure, by means of the sacrifice of Jesus, the Messiah.

HEBREWS 13:20,21 THE MESSAGE

May the words of my mouth and the meditation of my heart be pleasing in your sight, O Lord, my Rock and my Redeemer.

PSALM 19:14 NIV

EXAMPLE

David was a man who pleased the Lord. In fact, the Bible gives him this commendation:

"I've searched the land and found this David, son of Jesse. He's a man whose heart beats to my heart, a man who will do what I tell him."

ACTS 13:22 THE MESSAGE

What was David's "secret"? He understood and enjoyed the grace of God. He had deep love and respect for the Lord and a great desire to express that love in worship:

God — you're my God! I can't get enough of you! I've worked up such hunger and thirst for God, traveling across dry and weary deserts.
So here I am in the place of worship, eyes open, drinking in your strength and glory.
In your generous love I am really living at last!
My lips brim praises like fountains.
I bless you every time I take a breath; my arms wave like banners of praise to you.

PSALM 63:1-4 THE MESSAGE

Thank you! Everything in me says "Thank you!" Angels listen as I sing my thanks. I kneel in worship facing your holy temple and say it again: "Thank you!" Thank you for your love, thank you for your faithfulness.

PSALM 138:1,2 THE MESSAGE

Q: I JUST BLEW IT AGAIN, LORD.
AM I STILL SAVED?

A: In the past all of us lived like them, trying to please our sinful selves and doing all the
things our bodies and minds wanted. We
should have suffered God's anger because of
the way we were.... But God's mercy is great,
and he loved us very much. Though we were
spiritually dead because of the things we did
against God, he gave us new life with Christ.

EPHESIANS 2:3-5 NCV

INSTRUCTIONS

You have been saved by grace through believing. You did not save yourselves; it was a gift
from God. It was not the result of your own
efforts, so you cannot brag about it.

EPHESIANS 2:8,9 NCV

If you claim that God's promise is for those
who obey God's law and think they are "good

enough" in God's sight, then you are saying
that faith is useless.

ROMANS 4:14 NLT

Can't you see the central issue in all this? It is
not what you and I do.... It is what God is
doing, and he is creating something totally
new, a free life!

GALATIANS 6:15 THE MESSAGE

The fulfillment of God's promise depends
entirely on trusting God and his way, and then
simply embracing him and what he does.
God's promise arrives as pure gift. That's the
only way everyone can be sure to get in on it.

ROMANS 4:16 THE MESSAGE

PROMISES

God has given us eternal life, and this life is in
His Son. He who has the Son has life; he who
does not have the Son of God does not have
life. These things I have written to you who
believe in the name of the Son of God, that
you may know that you have eternal life, and
that you may continue to believe in the name
of the Son of God.

1 JOHN 5:11-13 NKJV

Yet to all who received him, to those who believed in his name, he gave the right to become children of God.

JOHN 1:12 NIV

I tell you the truth, whoever hears what I say and believes in the One who sent me has eternal life. That person will not be judged guilty but has already left death and entered life.

JOHN 5:24 NCV

"My sheep hear My voice, and I know them, and they follow Me; and I give eternal life to them, and they shall never perish; and no one will snatch them out of My hand."

JOHN 10:27,28 NASB

For it is God Who is all the while effectually at work in you — energizing and creating in you the power and desire — both to will and to work for His good pleasure and satisfaction and delight.

PHILIPPIANS 2:13 AMP

I will lead the blind by ways they have not known...I will turn the darkness into light before them and make the rough places smooth. These are the things I will do; I will

not forsake them.
                                        ISAIAH 42:16 NIV

For He Himself has said, "I will never leave
you nor forsake you."
                                        HEBREWS 13:5 NKJV

PRAYER

I pray for you constantly, asking God, the glorious Father of our Lord Jesus Christ, to give
you wisdom to see clearly and really understand who Christ is and all that he has done
for you. I pray that your hearts will be flooded
with light so that you can see something of the
future he has called you to share.... I pray that
you will begin to understand how incredibly
great his power is to help those who believe
him. It is that same mighty power that raised
Christ from the dead and seated him in the
place of honor at God's right hand in heaven.

                                    EPHESIANS 1:16-20 TLB

EXAMPLE

*Abraham received right standing with God by
faith, apart from any good works that he did. The
Bible calls him the "father of all people who*

embrace what God does for them" (Romans 4:11 THE MESSAGE).

Abraham never wavered in believing God's promise.... He was absolutely convinced that God was able to do anything he promised.

ROMANS 4:20,21 NLT

When everything was hopeless, Abraham believed anyway, deciding to live not on the basis of what he saw he couldn't do but on what God said he would do.... He didn't tiptoe around God's promise asking cautiously skeptical questions. He plunged into the promise and came up strong, ready for God, sure that God would make good on what he had said. That's why it is said, "Abraham was declared fit before God by trusting God to set him right."

ROMANS 4:17,20,22 THE MESSAGE

Q: WHAT ABOUT PRAYER?
IS THERE A "RIGHT" WAY
TO PRAY?

A: "This is what I want you to do: Ask the
Father for whatever is in keeping with the
things I've revealed to you. Ask in my name,
according to my will, and he'll most certainly
give it to you."   JOHN 16:23,24 THE MESSAGE

INSTRUCTIONS

Keep on asking, and you will be given what
you ask for. Keep on looking, and you will find.
Keep on knocking, and the door will be
opened. For everyone who asks, receives.
Everyone who seeks, finds. And the door is
opened to everyone who knocks. You parents
— if your children ask for a loaf of bread, do
you give them a stone instead? Or if they ask
for a fish, do you give them a snake? Of course
not! If you sinful people know how to give

good gifts to your children, how much more will your heavenly Father give good gifts to those who ask him.

MATTHEW 7:7-11 NLT

I am the vine, and you are the branches. If you stay joined to me, and I stay joined to you, then you will produce lots of fruit. But you cannot do anything without me.... Stay joined to me and let my teachings become part of you. Then you can pray for whatever you want, and your prayer will be answered.

JOHN 15:5,7 CEV

God is strong, and he wants you strong. So take everything the Master has set out for you, well-made weapons of the best materials. And put them to use so you will be able to stand up to everything the Devil throws your way. This is no afternoon athletic contest that we'll walk away from and forget about in a couple of hours. This is for keeps, a life-or-death fight to the finish against the Devil and all his angels.

Be prepared. You're up against far more than you can handle on your own. Take all the help you can get, every weapon God has issued, so that when it's all over but the shouting you'll still be on your feet.... God's Word is an *indispensable* weapon. In the same way, prayer is essential in this ongoing warfare. Pray hard and long.

EPHESIANS 6:10-18 THE MESSAGE

Never give up praying. And when you pray, keep alert and be thankful. COLOSSIANS 4:2 CEV

Always pray by the power of the Spirit.

EPHESIANS 6:18 CEV

The Holy Spirit helps us in our distress. For we don't even know what we should pray for, nor how we should pray. But the Holy Spirit prays for us with groanings that cannot be expressed in words. And the Father who knows all hearts knows what the Spirit is saying, for the Spirit pleads for us believers in harmony with God's own will. ROMANS 8:26,27 NLT

I will pray with the spirit, and I will also pray with the understanding.

1 CORINTHIANS 14:15 NKJV

PROMISES

The Lord is near to all who call upon Him, to all who call upon Him in truth. He will fulfill the desire of those who fear Him; He will also hear their cry and will save them.

PSALM 145:18,19 NASB

The eyes of the Lord are on the righteous, and His ears are open to their cry.... The righteous cry out, and the Lord hears, and delivers them out of all their troubles.

PSALM 34:15,17 NKJV

"Before they call, I will answer; and while they are still speaking, I will hear."

ISAIAH 65:24 NKJV

Then said the Lord to me... I am alert and active, watching over My word to perform it.

JEREMIAH 1:12 AMP

This is the confidence which we have before Him, that, if we ask anything according to His will, He hears us. And if we know that He hears us in whatever we ask, we know that we have the requests which we have asked from Him.

1 JOHN 5:14,15 NASB

"Again, I tell you that if two of you on earth agree about anything you ask for, it will be done for you by my Father in heaven. For where two or three come together in my name, there am I with them."

MATTHEW 18:19,20 NIV

And Jesus replying said to them, Have faith in God (constantly). Truly, I tell you, whoever says to this mountain, Be lifted up and thrown into the sea! and does not doubt at all in his heart, but believes that what he says will take place, it will be done for him. For this reason I am telling you, whatever you ask for in prayer, believe — trust and be confident — that it is granted to you, and you will [get it].

MARK 11:22-24 AMP

Let us then fearlessly and confidently and boldly draw near to the throne of grace...that we may receive mercy...and find grace to help in good time for every need — appropriate help and well-timed help, coming just when we need it.

HEBREWS 4:16 AMP

The earnest (heartfelt, continued) prayer of a righteous man makes tremendous power available — dynamic in its working.

JAMES 5:16 AMP

With God's power working in us, God can do

much, much more than anything we can ask or
imagine.

EPHESIANS 3:20 NCV

PRAYERS

I pray that Christ will live in your hearts by
faith and that your life will be strong in love and
be built on love. And I pray that you...will have
the power to understand the greatness of
Christ's love — how wide and how long and
how high and how deep that love is. Christ's
love is greater than anyone can ever know, but I
pray that you will be able to know that love.
Then you can be filled with the fullness of God.

EPHESIANS 3:17-19 NCV

We ask God to give you a complete understanding of what he wants to do in your lives,
and we ask him to make you wise with spiritual
wisdom. Then the way you live will always
honor and please the Lord, and you will continually do good, kind things for others...We also
pray that you will be strengthened with his glorious power so that you will have all the patience
and endurance you need. May you be filled with
joy, always thanking the Father.

COLOSSIANS 1:9-12 NLT

BIBLE REFERENCES

Scripture references marked KJV are taken from the *King James Version* of the Bible.

Scripture references marked NKJV are taken from the *New King James Version.* Copyright © 1979, 1980, 1982 by Thomas Nelson, Inc. Used by permission. All rights reserved.

Scripture references marked NASB are taken from the NEW AMERICAN STANDARD BIBLE, Copyright © 1960, 1962, 1963, 1968, 1971, 1972, 1973, 1975, 1977, 1988, 1995 by The Lockman Foundation. Used by permission.

Scripture quotations marked NIV are taken from the HOLY BIBLE, NEW INTERNATIONAL VERSION®. NIV®. Copyright © 1973, 1978, 1984 by the International Bible Society. Used by permission of Zondervan Publishing House. All rights reserved.

Scripture references marked THE MESSAGE are taken from *THE MESSAGE.* Copyright © by Eugene H. Peterson, 1993, 1994, 1995. Used by permission of NavPress Publishing Group.

Scripture references marked NLT are taken from the *Holy Bible, New Living Translation,* copyright © 1996. Used by permission of Tyndale House Publishers, Inc., Wheaton, Illinois 60189. All rights reserved.

Scripture references marked NCV are taken from *The Holy Bible, New Century Version,* copyright © 1987, 1988, 1991 by Word Publishing, Nashville, Tennessee 37214. Used by permission.